CW01468096

QUEENS OF
R&B

G:

Published in 2026
by Gemini Gift Books
Part of Gemini Books Group

Based in Woodbridge and London

Marine House, Tide Mill Way,
Woodbridge, Suffolk IP12 1AP
United Kingdom

www.geminibooks.com

Text and design © 2026 Gemini Gift Books Ltd

ISBN 978-1-78675-200-0

All rights reserved. No part of this publication may be reproduced in any form or by any means – electronic, mechanical, photocopying, recording or otherwise – or stored in any retrieval system of any nature without prior written permission from the copyright holders.

A CIP catalogue record for this book is available from the British Library.

Manufacturer's EU Representative: Eurolink Compliance Limited, 25 Herbert Place, Dublin, D02 AY86, Republic of Ireland. admin@eurolink-europe.ie

Disclaimer: The book is a guidebook purely for information and entertainment purposes only. All trademarks, individual & company names, brand names, registered names, quotations, celebrity names, logos, dialogues and catchphrases used or cited in this book are the property of their respective owners. The publisher does not assume and hereby disclaim any liability to any party for any loss, damage or disruption caused by errors or omissions, whether such errors or omissions result from negligence, accident, or any other cause. This book is an unofficial and unauthorized publication by Gemini Gift Books Ltd and has not been licensed, approved, sponsored or endorsed by the artists mentioned in this book or any other person or entity.

Printed in China

10 9 8 7 6 5 4 3 2 1

QUEENS OF R&B

KIANA FITZGERALD

G:

CONTENTS

INTRODUCTION

Rhythm and blues is the living, breathing foundation of contemporary music. The genre itself may not have been acknowledged or even identified on a public platform until the mid-twentieth century, but every moment – and movement – since then has proven that R&B is the driving factor behind the exponential progress that's been made within the music industry.

The US-based education and research entity, the Smithsonian Center for Folklife & Cultural Heritage, offers this definition of R&B: "A distinctly African American music drawing from the deep tributaries of African American expressive culture, it is an amalgam of jump blues, big band swing, gospel, boogie, and blues that was initially developed during a thirty-year period that bridges the era of legally sanctioned racial segregation, international conflicts, and the struggle for civil rights."

As a journalist at the US music industry magazine *Billboard* during the '40s, Jerry Wexler coined the term "rhythm and blues" to describe the earthy, soulful music being created by Black artists: "'Race' was a common term then, a self-referral used by Blacks … On the other hand, 'Race Records' didn't sit well … I came up with a handle I thought suited the music well – 'rhythm and blues' … [It was] a label more appropriate to more enlightened times." The fact that a white man was the source of the terminology that would come to shape decades of Black-made music speaks to the systemic barriers that those musicians faced.

> **I came up with a handle I thought suited the music well – 'rhythm and blues'… [It was] a label more appropriate to more enlightened times.**
>
> **JERRY WEXLER**

Ruth Brown, a fierce singer who gained the title Miss Rhythm in the '40s and '50s, eventually became known as the Queen of R&B. Her vocal stylistic work would later influence musicians of every colour. Brown was a rollicking singer, as heard on her simmering 1953 signature song 'Mama He Treats Your Daughter Mean.' As one of the earliest adopters of rhythm

Legendary rhythm and blues singer Ruth Brown became known as the queen of R&B in the 1950s.

Big Mama Thornton (above and right), a pioneer of rock and roll in the 1950s, was first known as a progenitor of rhythm and blues.

and blues, Brown fully captured the essence of Black liberation, struggle, joy and celebration and often topped the US Billboard R&B chart.

By the '50s, R&B transformed, shifting from doo-wop (The Flamingos, The Drifters) to outright rock and roll (Chuck Berry, Little Richard). Big Mama Thornton, a pioneer of rock and roll, was first known as a progenitor of rhythm and blues. 'Hound Dog', written specifically for her by Jerry Leiber and Mike Stoller, became Thornton's biggest hit, selling over half a million copies and sitting atop the Billboard R&B chart for seven weeks in 1953.

The definition of 'rhythm and blues' has transformed over time. It was frequently applied to blues records in the early '50s, but by the mid-1950s, after the proliferation of rock and roll, "R&B" was used to describe music styles that were influenced by electric blues, in addition to gospel and soul music. In the mid-to-late twentieth century, from the '60s to the '70s, British bands such as The Rolling Stones and The Animals were referred to and promoted as R&B bands, alongside Motown acts like The Supremes and The Temptations. By the end of the '70s, R&B was used to describe soul and funk acts, like James Brown and Earth, Wind & Fire. In the '80s, R&B became a vehicle for pop superstardom: Michael Jackson, Janet Jackson and Whitney Houston evolved into the most well-known acts in modern history, using rhythm and blues as the white-hot flame to their chart-topping rocket ships. Subgenres such as New Jack Swing and Adult Contemporary R&B unleashed the possibility of varied instances of rhythm and blues.

The 1990s are by far considered the Golden Era of R&B. With a plethora of converging acts, from the Queen of Hip-Hop Soul Mary J. Blige to the Princess of R&B Aaliyah, the genre was propelled by women who spoke truth to power and applied emotive vulnerability to their – at times harsh, at times beautiful – realities. This era also paved the way for hip-hop collaborations, an intertwining that became essential to both genres in the 2000s and still is today. Acts like Beyoncé, Ciara and Alicia Keys brought R&B back to the pop world, learning from the accomplishments of their predecessors like Houston, who worked directly with Keys. The 2010s and 2020s have set the scene for R&B to be everything it has touched, all at once: as freely energetic as rock and roll, as infectiously charming as pop, as thrillingly catchy as hip-hop, and as true to form as the beating heart of rhythm and blues itself.

In the music industry writ large, the producer is just as important a factor as the vocalist and R&B is no different. From Missy 'Misdemeanor' Elliott (702, Aaliyah, SWV, Total) to Kenneth 'Babyface' Edmonds (Whitney Houston, TLC, Mary J. Blige) and Jimmy Jam and Terry Lewis (Janet Jackson, Mariah Carey, Cherrelle) to Rodney 'Darkchild' Jerkins (Brandy, Destiny's Child, Monica), the composers and arrangers, songwriters and instrumentalists just out of view are equally key to the vivacity and theatricality of R&B.

The R&B queens profiled in this book include pop supernovas (Whitney Houston, Mariah Carey, SZA), R&B mainstays (Mary J. Blige, Ashanti, H.E.R.) and boundary pushers (Janet Jackson, Aaliyah, Destiny's Child, Brandy). Whether longevity was achieved or careers cut tragically short, each of these women impacted R&B in a major way. Their contributions are just as profound as the genre itself and their lasting impact as individuals, while larger than life, feels personal to every fan who presses play on their records.

Jackson ranks alongside other boundary pushers and pop supernovas as a queen of R&B.

JANET
JACKSON

Janet Jackson was born to be influential. The youngest of ten children in the sprawling, musically gifted and exceedingly trained Jackson family, the singer-songwriter, actress and dancer had an unprecedented opportunity to watch her older brothers seek and attain success as The Jackson 5 when she was a small child. Of course, her big brother Michael would go on to become The King of Pop, one of the most revered musicians of all time, so that meant Janet had to carve out a lane of her very own. "When you have the last name Jackson, there's a certain microscope that [critics] want to use with that," Jackson said in the four-part *Janet Jackson.* documentary series released in 2022.

Born Janet Damita Jo Jackson in Gary, Indiana in 1966, Jackson grew up knowing that her older siblings were focused on music, but she didn't necessarily want to join the family trade. Under the strict guidance of their father and mother Joe and Katherine Jackson, but most especially Joe, the Jackson children thrived creatively and professionally. After moving to the affluent, white suburb of Encino, Los Angeles, the Jacksons had an at-home studio, where they wrote, produced and taped their fleeting musical concepts. One day, Janet had an idea, so she created a song entirely on her own, even playing all the parts. "Like a genius, I left the tape on the machine and when I came home from school I was so embarrassed," Jackson said in the February 2022 issue of *Allure*. 'They were listening

" I knew that I had to take control of my life.
JANET JACKSON

to the song; my father, some of my brothers. I was so embarrassed. And that's when my father said, 'I think you should become a performer.' I said, 'No, no, no, no, no! You don't understand. I want to go to school. I want to go to college and study business law and support myself by acting.' That's how it all started."

The first time Janet Jackson performed on stage was in Las Vegas at age seven. Along with her siblings, Jackson performed two to three weeks at a time, two shows a night. In 1976, she began acting in *The Jacksons*, the first variety show that featured a cast that was entirely made up of siblings, as well as the first African American family. By the following year, she was starring as Penny Gordon Woods in the sitcom

Janet was the youngest of ten children in the sprawling, musically gifted and exceedingly trained Jackson family.

MARLO
ON
Smile
TOYA
REBE
HELLO
RANDY
J-
JACKIE
MIKE
Hi
MIKE
J-5
JANET
BUD
DADDY
HI

Good Times, her breakout role and proper introduction to the world. In addition to acting, Jackson, at her father's behest, began working on her own music. The Jackson brothers had fired Joe as their manager by this point, so he focused all of his attention on Janet, closely controlling her image and sound in the same managerial role.

Janet Jackson's debut, self-titled 1982 album was driven by soul, pop, funk and Motown, and shared thematic and sonic similarities to works by Michael and The Jackson 5. Janet delicately balanced ballads ('Love And My Best Friend', 'Forever Yours') with uptempo jams ('Say You Do', 'Young Love'), settling in a decidedly saccharine spot that she would replicate with her 1984 follow-up *Dream Street*. These early, bubblegum-soul albums didn't quite mesh with audiences and Janet felt

she was being stifled as an artist – she was being told what to make and how to make it, not crafting albums that she herself wanted to write and produce. "I knew that I had to take control of my life," Jackson said in the 2022 documentary. "I wanted my own identity. I wanted to go on my own."

With the 1986 release of *Control*, Jackson reinvented herself. Before she began work on the album, Janet effectively broke away from her father, who had managed all aspects of her nascent career until that point. With an independent, intentional goal in mind, Jackson set about finding her musical partners in crime. The esteemed production duo Jimmy Jam and Terry Lewis (members of the Prince-approved band The Time) were up for the challenge, which was to drastically redirect Janet's life and career. "It was apparent that nobody had really asked her opinion about what she wanted to sing about," Jimmy Jam said in the

Jackson felt stifled early on in her career and in later years shared her desire to forge her own path.

same documentary. "We wanted her to make *her* record. And I think it was like a revelation to her." Jackson set the tone of the entire project on the album intro, which doubled as the title track: "This is a story about control – my control," Jackson states clearly. "Control of what I say, and control of what I do. And this time, I'm gonna do it *my* way."

Due to its forthright energy and feminist perspective, *Control* was seen as bold for Janet Jackson, who was 19 at the time of its release. Sonically, Jimmy Jam and Terry Lewis broadened Jackson's sound, with less traditional musicality, more open space, cold, industrial elements and tighter rhythms. They also fused hip-hop and R&B undertones, perhaps unintentionally but directly influencing the development of

> " I just want my music and my dance to catch the audience's attention and to hold it long enough for them to listen to the lyrics.
> **JANET JACKSON**

New Jack Swing. Jackson herself became more emboldened in her delivery, with a focus on empowering herself and her female listeners. She stood up for herself in a purposeful way, demanding respect through songs that were as confrontational (the chastising 'Nasty', the utterly fed-up 'What Have You Done For Me Lately') as they were uninhibited (the deceptively dulcet 'The Pleasure Principle', the oft-sampled 'Funny How Time Flies (When You're Having Fun)'). 'When I Think of You', a more sentimental, pop-adjacent track, became Jackson's first No. 1 hit on the Billboard Hot 100.

A wildly successful change of pace, *Control*, her first album to top the Billboard 200, essentially turned Jackson into an overnight pop

With 1986's *Control*, Jackson broke away from her father's guiding hand, partnered with producers Jimmy Jam and Terry Lewis and ultimately took charge of her career.

star. Her label, A&M, wanted a direct sequel to the instant classic, but Jackson was more interested in a creative shift: rather than looking inward, she chose to gaze out meaningfully at the troubled world around her. A swell of crimes and tragedies were dominating the news and other media, and Jackson wanted to provide a unifying message that would help the masses to cope, and more determinedly, come together.

Partnering again with Jimmy Jam and Terry Lewis, Jackson went to work constructing the socially conscious 1989 album *Rhythm Nation 1814*, a project that saw Jackson experimenting grandly with New Jack Swing, as well as other styles like pop, dance and rock. Ambitious and aware, the album was also Jackson's opportunity to ramp up her dance style and choreography, which she began exploring in earnest during *Control*. "I know an album or a song can't change the world," Jackson told *USA Today* in 1989. "I just want my music and my dance to catch

the audience's attention and to hold it long enough for them to listen to the lyrics."

The iconic 'Rhythm Nation' music video established Jackson's vision, underscored by galvanizing lyrics like, "Join voices in protest to social injustice / A generation full of courage, come forth with me." Backed by a diverse mix of dancers, Jackson performed intricate steps in a dystopian warehouse in black-and-white visuals and sang about eradicating "colour lines" and coming together as a people. In 2011, *Rolling Stone* noted that the music video "set the template for hundreds of videos to come in the '90s and aughts." As popular as 'Rhythm Nation' was, there were plenty of other moments on the

With the groundbreaking, disruptive album *Rhythm Nation 1814*, Jackson transformed her image and career yet again.

album that connected with listeners. To date, Jackson remains the sole artist in Billboard chart history to have seven singles from one album peak within the top five positions: the No. 1 hits 'Miss You Much', 'Escapade', 'Black Cat' and 'Love Will Never Do (Without You)', as well as 'Rhythm Nation', 'Alright' and 'Come Back to Me'. This achievement is something not even her older brother Michael accomplished in his career, though Janet never considered herself to be in competition with him. Additionally, Jackson's Rhythm Nation World Tour 1990 became the most successful debut tour in history, raking in $28 million (around $68 million today) generated from over 110 shows.

Jackson's contract with her first label A&M was up after *Rhythm Nation 1814* and a high-profile bidding war ensued. She wound up signing a deal with Virgin Records, estimated to be for between $40–50 million (around $93–117 million today), which made her the world's highest paid musical act at the time. Her highly anticipated follow-up, 1993's *janet.*, was yet another marked departure from what was expected of her, even as far back as her first eponymous album, *Janet Jackson*. Back then, Jackson was opposed to having her last name on her debut, as she didn't want to have to rely on her family's myriad successes to build her own career. With *janet.*, her first album to outright debut at No. 1 on the Billboard 200, she was finally able to reclaim her own name and present it in a way that benefitted her.

Instead of following the relatively conservative path that she had been paving by way of her recent albums, *janet.* was a deep dive into erotic R&B. With laid-back grooves like the No. 1 single 'That's The Way Loves Goes' and overtly sensuous songs like 'Any Time, Any Place', Jackson transitioned from pop star to sex icon, while still retaining

Jackson made history with seven top five singles from one album and the most successful debut tour ever, ultimately leading to a label bidding war and a record-breaking contract.

her widespread popularity. Musically, Jackson worked with Jimmy Jam and Terry Lewis, alongside multi-instrumentalist Jellybean Johnson, to refine a sleek R&B sound that served as the foundation of the album. 'Again', a piano-driven ballad that also hit No. 1, saw Jackson working through an imperfect relationship, but ultimately choosing to believe in love again. The song was featured during the closing scenes of *Poetic Justice*, a 1993 film that Jackson co-starred in with Tupac Shakur; 'Again' was nominated for an Academy Award for Best Original Song.

The Velvet Rope followed in 1997, again debuting at No. 1. It presented a Janet Jackson who had experienced a successful, but tumultuous life thus far – she faced raging body image issues and depression, and had also been in challenging relationships, romantically and within her family. "I had my ways of hiding my pain," she said in the December 1997 issue of *Ebony*. "Laughing when there was nothing to laugh at; smiling when there wasn't anything to smile about. That was just my way of getting through life. Pretending like everything was okay. I guess I did it so well that I really began to believe it. I fooled myself."

> **As the youngest in the family, I was determined to make it on my own.**
>
> **JANET JACKSON**

Jackson confronted these issues head-on with *The Velvet Rope*, through songs like the international No. 1 house-pop/dance megahit 'Together Again' that invokes the memory of a friend who passed away due to AIDS, and the optimistically reflective, Joni Mitchell-sampling 'Got 'Til It's Gone', which won the 1998 Grammy Award for Best Short Form Music Video.

Jackson adapted well in the aughts, releasing the remarkably upbeat *All For You* in 2001; the title track, propelled by a mix of pop, R&B, funk and disco, hit No. 1 and won Best Dance Recording at the 2002

Grammys. The sweet and sunny 'Someone To Call My Lover' reached No. 3 and was selected by reviewers as the album's strongest song. In February 2004, Jackson performed at the Super Bowl XXXVIII halftime show. Justin Timberlake's unintentional exposure of her right breast was a hyper-sensationalized moment that lasted less than one second, but it nearly cost Jackson her career. She was publicly blacklisted and her forthcoming album, *Damita Jo*, was severely impacted. Even so, critics insisted that the project – led by the Prince-inspired, guitar-riff-heavy single 'Just A Little While', released the day after the Super Bowl – would have performed well if not for the industry-wide backlash.

Jackson co-starred in the 1993 film *Poetic Justice* alongside the late Tupac Shakur.

Resilient and determined, Jackson continued releasing new material, including 2006's *20 Y.O.* (a 20-year celebration of *Control*) and 2008's *Discipline*, whose highlights include the dynamic, electro-R&B single 'Feedback' and the digitally mellifluous 'Rock With U'. Seven years later, Jackson released *Unbreakable*, a well-formed, explorative project that featured her collaborating with new talent ('No Sleeep' with North Carolina MC J. Cole) and cemented legends alike ('BURNITUP!' with Missy Elliott). As of the mid-2020s, Jackson remains a beloved live performance artist, continuing her massively influential tours and Vegas residencies and delighting her fans that span across generations.

Janet Jackson

ALBUMS:

Janet Jackson (1982)
Dream Street (1984)
Control (1986)
Janet Jackson's Rhythm Nation 1814 (1989)
janet. (1993)
The Velvet Rope (1997)
All for You (2001)
Damita Jo (2004)
20 Y.O. (2006)
Discipline (2008)
Unbreakable (2015)

SONGS:

'Young Love' (1982)
'Say You Do' (1982)
'What Have You Done For Me Lately' (1986)
'Nasty' (1986)
'When I Think of You' (1986)
'Control' (1986)
'The Pleasure Principle' (1986)
'Funny How Time Flies (When You're Having Fun)' (1986)
'Miss You Much' (1989)
'Rhythm Nation' (1989)
'Escapade' (1990)
'Alright' (1990)
'Come Back to Me' (1990)
'Black Cat' (1990)
'Love Will Never Do (Without You)' (1990)
'That's the Way Love Goes' (1993)
'Again' (1993)
'Any Time, Any Place' (1994)
'Got 'Til It's Gone' (1997)
'Together Again' (1997)
'Doesn't Really Matter' (2000)
'All for You' (2001)
'Someone To Call My Lover' (2001)
'Just A Little While' (2004)
'Feedback' (2007)
'Rock With U' (2008)
'No Sleeep' featuring J. Cole (2015)
'BURNITUP!' with Missy Elliott (2015)

Without Janet Jackson, there would be no alternative R&B, and no contemporary Pop&B. As such, there would be no Britney Spears, no Destiny's Child or Beyoncé, no J. Lo, no Christina Aguilera, no Aaliyah, no Ciara, no Rihanna – not even Usher, Justin Timberlake or NSYNC could escape the long shadow cast by Jackson.

In 2019, Janet Jackson joined her older brothers of The Jackson 5 in the Rock & Roll Hall of Fame, a recognition that many considered to be long overdue. "I witnessed, along with the rest of the world, my family's extraordinary impact on popular culture," Janet said during her induction speech. "Not just in America, but all around the globe. The entire globe. And as the youngest in the family, I was determined to make it on my own. I wanted to stand on my own two feet. But never in a million years did I expect to follow in their footsteps. Tonight, your baby sister has made it."

Despite facing backlash after the 2004 Super Bowl controversy, Jackson has remained resilient, influencing countless artists across genres and generations.

JANET JACKSON

JANET JACKSON, 'THAT'S THE WAY LOVE GOES'

Release date: April 20, 1993
Album: *janet.*
Recorded: 1993
Label: Virgin
Studio: Flyte Tyme (Minnesota)
Songwriters: Janet Jackson, James 'Jimmy Jam' Harris III, Terry Lewis
Billboard Hot 100: 1
UK Singles Chart: 2

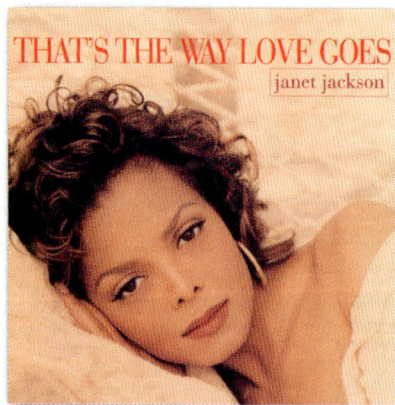

Critical Acclaim

The lead single of 1993's *janet.*, a highly anticipated follow-up to Jackson's socially conscious 1989 album *Rhythm Nation 1814*, 'That's the Way Love Goes' was a marked departure from what was expected of her. Instead of following the relatively conservative path that she had been paving by way of her recent music, 'That's The Way Loves Goes' was a deep dive into laid-back grooves and erotic R&B. At this moment, Jackson transitioned from pop star to sex icon, while still retaining her widespread popularity.

Recording

According to co-producer Jimmy Jam, *janet.* was a deviation from *Rhythm Nation* because all of the collaborators were happy and in love. 'That's the Way Love Goes' was Jackson's way of introducing listeners to her new way of being. Shortly before taking a holiday break from working on *janet.*, Jackson asked Jam if he would make her a cassette of all the productions Harris and Terry Lewis had been working on. Upon returning from vacation, Jackson revealed she had fallen in love with the soundscape of 'That's the Way Love Goes' and wanted to work on it immediately. The song contains samples of 'Impeach the President' by The Honey Drippers and 'Papa Don't Take No Mess' by James Brown.

Legacy

'That's the Way Love Goes' topped the *Billboard* Hot 100 for eight weeks and received the 1993 Grammy Award for Best R&B Song. Artists such as Britney Spears, Destiny's Child and Alicia Keys have cited the song and video as a direct inspiration. What began as a reintroduction of Janet Jackson transformed into a sexual awakening for American culture at large.

Remixes

The official mixes and remixes of 'That's the Way Love Goes' include CJ R&B 7" Mix, Macapella and We Aimsta Win Mix 2.

Covers

- **1998, Kirk Whalum** - The jazz saxophonist recorded an instrumental version on his album *For You*.
- **2001, NSYNC** - Janet Jackson was the first artist honoured on MTV's 'Icon' series. NSYNC paid homage by rerecording the song and recreating its music video.
- **Bruno Mars** - During his concerts in the early to mid-2010s, Mars performed 'That's the Way Loves Goes' in part.

WHITNEY
HOUSTON

Across the history of recorded music, few artists are as revered as Whitney Houston. Known simply as 'the Voice', Houston broke through multiple social and racial barriers and shattered numerous records throughout her career, imbuing her music with an effortless effervescence that at any moment could transform into a powerful swell of emotion.

Before Whitney was a pop culture icon, she was welcomed into a gifted musical family through what her father, John Houston, considered osmosis. "You can't remember the first time you were in a recording studio, because your mother was pregnant with you," he told Whitney during an interview with *People* in December 1985, laughing at the memory in the moment. Born in 1963 in Newark, New Jersey, Whitney Elizabeth Houston's path was all but set as the daughter of Cissy Houston, herself a singer, who became known as a member of the Drinkards gospel quartet and the R&B group The Sweet Inspirations. In the latter, Cissy had the opportunity

I was taught to listen and observe.
WHITNEY HOUSTON

to work as a backing singer for a considerable list of music innovators, from Aretha Franklin to Elvis Presley. Whitney often sat in on recording sessions, soaking in knowledge from some of the industry's most resilient voices. "Being around people like Aretha Franklin and Gladys Knight, Dionne Warwick and Roberta Flack, all these greats, I was taught to listen and observe," Whitney told *Rolling Stone* in June 1993. "It had a great impact on me as a singer, as a performer, as a musician. Growing up around it, you just can't help it. I identified with it immediately. It was something that was so natural to me that when I started singing, it was almost like speaking."

"I think so much about what it must have been like for Whitney at four and five and six years old, to be sitting in a studio, understanding that I have this voice, and I want to sing like my mom," Gerrick Kennedy, author of the 2022 biography *Didn't We Almost Have it All: In Defense of Whitney Houston*, told KCRW in February 2022. "And this is something I'm really, really, really liking right now. But you are watching your mom sing with Aretha Franklin. I mean, just the image of that on its own gives

me chills. And I thought so much about what we learn through osmosis. When we think about kids in the womb, just the level of education that was being lavished upon this young woman, this young girl."

That high-calibre group of influences included her cousin, R&B great Dionne Warwick – but it was Aretha Franklin, in particular, who became

Houston was immersed in music from birth and observed some of the greatest voices in intimate settings, including Aretha Franklin.

Whitney's go-to model for vocal excellence. "When I heard Aretha, I could feel her emotional delivery so clearly," Whitney told *People*. "It came from down deep within. That's what I wanted to do." Inspired by her mother Cissy, and the artists she'd been exposed to, Whitney soon began trying her own hand at singing. "I'd hear all this hollering and screaming down in the basement," John Houston said. "Whitney'd be down there with one of Cissy's microphones singing along with Chaka Khan and Aretha records. I knew her mother was training her, but I wasn't paying much attention. One day Cissy said, 'Your baby is soloing in church for the first time this Sunday. Be there.' What I heard that day was the voice of a young woman coming from the throat of a 12-year-old child. It blew my mind."

Whitney cut her teeth as a singer in the New Hope Baptist Church in Newark, where her mother served as choir minister. "I would close my eyes [like this] and I'd sing," Whitney told Diane Sawyer on a Special Edition of ABC Primetime in November 2002. "I was so afraid when I'd sing. And when I would open my eyes, the people would be what we call 'Holy Ghost fired out.' They would be in such [a] spirit of praise, I think I knew then that it was an infectious thing that God had given me." By the late '70s, Whitney was sharing a stage – and a spotlight – with her mother at nightclubs and cabarets across New York. According to Whitney's mother, Luther Vandross wanted to produce her as a solo artist when she was 15, but Cissy and John knew the industry would be fast and furious. "I wanted her to finish school first, because I knew if she got started in the business, there'd be no stopping her," Cissy told *People*.

Even so, Whitney's magnetism to the music world was irrepressible. Before graduating high school in 1981, she began singing background for Chaka Khan and Lou Rawls. By 1983, Clive Davis, Chairman and

Houston trained her voice in a variety of settings, from church performances to nightclub and cabaret sets with her mother.

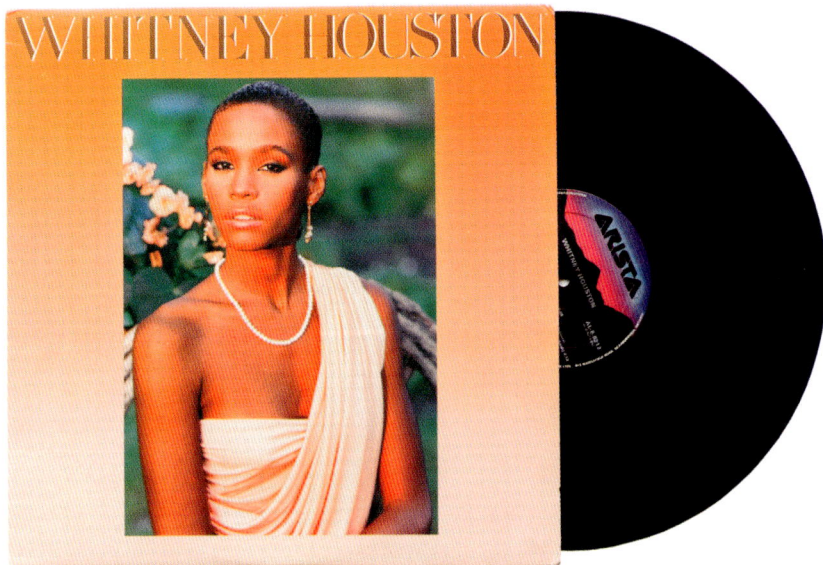

> **"** My success happened so quickly that when I first came out, Black people felt 'she belongs to us.'

WHITNEY HOUSTON

CEO of Arista Records, caught wind of Whitney's talent and signed her on the spot. "Clive is a master at pop music," Kenneth Reynolds, former marketing executive at Arista Records, said in *Whitney: Can I Be Me (2018)*. "He had a vision for a pop artist. He tried to do it with Dionne and Aretha, but they were far too established in their career, as to who they were. And along comes Whitney, who was so mouldable, and she was the perfect vehicle for his foolproof vision." From early on, it was decided that Whitney's sound would be universal and virtually colourless. "Her music was deliberately pop," Reynolds said. "Anything that was too Black sounding was sent back to the studio. And to say 'Black sounding', in case you have a problem with that, it's to say that it's too George Clinton. It's too Funkadelic. It's just too R&B. … We don't want a female James Brown."

The sound that Clive Davis and Arista Records landed on was massively emotive and intentionally unifying. Whitney's self-titled debut was released in 1985 and it sparkled with deeply felt balladry (the Grammy-winning 'Saving All My Love for You') as much as it leaned on Whitney's pop-soul sensibilities and her early exploration of dance music ('How Will I Know'). These two singles, combined with 'Greatest Love of All', a George Benson cover with inspirational and uplifting messaging, gave Whitney Houston her first three No. 1 hits on the Billboard Hot 100. This made her self-titled album the first debut and the first album by a solo female artist to produce three No. 1 singles in the US. Internationally, the album topped many charts, including Canada, Norway, Sweden and Australia and hit No. 2 in the UK, Switzerland and Germany. It was the bestselling debut album by a solo artist, as well as one of the bestselling albums of all time, eventually earning a 14 times platinum certification.

Her follow-up album, 1987's *Whitney*, debuted at No. 1 on the Billboard 200 chart, making Houston the first female artist to ever debut at No. 1 in the US. With this album, Whitney also became the first solo Black female artist to have a No. 1 album in the UK. *Whitney* was home to the Grammy-winning smash hit 'I Wanna Dance with Somebody (Who Loves Me)', the downtempo ballad 'Didn't We Almost Have It All', the rock-infused electro jam 'So Emotional' and another heartrending serenade 'Where Do Broken Hearts Go' – all of which peaked at No. 1 on the Billboard Hot 100. These four songs, combined with the three No. 1 hits from her debut, gave Whitney an unprecedented, consecutive seven-single run atop the chart. At the time of writing, Whitney remains the only artist to have ever achieved this feat, surpassing acts like The Beatles and the Bee Gees. "Whitney was at the top of the chart," Doug Daniel, Arista R&B promotions executive, said in *Whitney: Can I Be Me*.

Houston's rise to superstardom was powered by Clive Davis's pop-focused vision for her first two albums, which earned her seven consecutive No. 1 hits.

"She had like four or five, six, seven, consecutive No. 1 records. These were pop records, they were massive. She was everywhere. And to the Black ear, these records didn't have a natural feel. These records were not natural R&B records. So for the Black audience, the perspective was in the community that Whitney had sold out."

"My success happened so quickly that when I first came out, Black people felt 'she belongs to us,'" Whitney told *Ebony* in May 1991. "And then all of a sudden the big success came and they felt I wasn't theirs anymore, that I wasn't within their reach. It was felt that I was making myself more accessible to whites, but I wasn't." Despite the difficulty connecting with the Black audience, Whitney's work was built upon an undeniably Black experience. Even so, listeners were restrictive in how that experience was presented. "There was this idea that she should be singing a particular type of music," author Gerrick Kennedy told KCRW.

Houston collaborated with Mariah Carey, deemed by many as her vocal successor, for *The Prince of Egypt* soundtrack.

"And so when it became these really softer ballads that lean to the pop side, it was: 'Well, I don't understand why this person is singing this. Why aren't they doing more deep, deep, deep soul?' Even though her first two albums before, there was a direct shift into, 'Let's make harder R&B,' there was still R&B on both those records. It's still rooted in R&B; it's still rooted in soul. She never departed from any of that. She never departed from the ways in which she sang in the church, even when she was doing those pop records. And I think that was also something, that it took a long time for everybody to really connect with: the fact that she was really pushing a tradition of singing into mainstream pop music. And being the first means that yes, there [are] going to be people who don't understand it."

After Whitney's name was booed at the 1989 Soul Train Music Awards during a nominee segment, the singer had had enough and was ready for a change. "Whitney insisted they crossed her back over to Black music," Houston's saxophonist Kirk Whalum said in *Whitney: Can I Be Me*. "*I'm Your Baby Tonight* was not a record that Clive Davis wanted to make, but she said, 'I'm not making another record like you want. I'm gonna

do *me* now.'" "I don't ever want to be in a realm where I'm caught in a mould that I can't get out [of]," Whitney told Diane Sawyer in 2002. "Ever, that's over. I'm beyond it." Songs like the title track of 1990's *I'm Your Baby Tonight* and 'All The Man That I Need' highlighted a more soulful sound, with Whitney's masterful voice threading the needle of expectation.

In November 1992, Whitney made her film debut in *The Bodyguard*, co-starring alongside Oscar-winning actor/director Kevin Costner, who hand-picked her for the role. "I was scared," Whitney told *Rolling Stone* in 1993. "It took me two years to decide to do it. I kind of waited too long for Kevin. I think it got on his nerves. He called me one day and said, 'Listen, are you going to do this movie with me or not?' I told him about my fears. I said, 'I'm afraid. I don't want to go out there and fall.' And he said: 'I promise you I will not let you fall. I will help you.' And he did." *The Bodyguard* was a box office success, raking in more than $400 million. The lead single of the soundtrack, Whitney's world-shifting cover of Dolly Parton's 'I Will Always Love You', peaked at No. 1 for a then record-breaking 14 weeks, and became the biggest selling single by a female artist in history. "I think Dolly Parton is a hell of a writer and a hell of a singer," Whitney told *Rolling Stone*. "I was concerned when I sang her song how she'd feel about it, in terms of the arrangement, my licks, my flavor. When she said she was floored, that meant so much to me."

David Foster, producer of 'I Will Always Love You', initially had a different vision for the song. "Kevin Costner had said to me, 'When she sings that song in the first chorus, I want it to be with no music,'" Foster said in *Whitney: Can I Be Me*. "And I said, 'Kevin, that's so stupid. No music, are you kidding me? We're trying to get on radio?' And I'm standing there and she goes, '*If, I…*' And it was like, 'Oh my God, are you kidding me? This is the most incredible thing I've ever seen in my life.' And my demo did not include that. I had music right from the start. And from that second on, I knew that the only way that record could ever be that way was with that a capella opening. It was just one of the most breathtaking things I've ever been part of, and it wasn't even my doing, it was Kevin Costner." 'I Will Always Love You' went on to win Record of the Year and Best Female Pop Vocal Performance at the 1994 Grammy Awards. Diamond-certified by the Recording Industry Association of America (RIAA) in the US, the song was also internationally beloved, topping the singles charts in at least 34 countries, including the Eurochart Hot 100 Singles, where it spent 13 weeks at the top. In 2019, the Library of Congress added Houston's version to the National Recording Registry. *The Bodyguard* soundtrack won the Grammy for Album of the Year and has been certified 18 times platinum, making it the biggest selling motion picture soundtrack of all time with nearly 50 million copies sold worldwide.

Whitney's film career continued with the 1995 Forest Whitaker-directed *Waiting to Exhale*, which saw Whitney co-starring

On January 27, 1991, during the Persian Gulf War, Houston sang the National Anthem at the pregame show of Super Bowl XXV.

alongside Angela Bassett, Loretta Devine and Lela Rochon. Houston also contributed to the Kenneth 'Babyface' Edmonds-helmed R&B soundtrack, including the No. 1 R&B and No. 1 Hot 100 hit 'Exhale (Shoop Shoop)'. *The Preacher's Wife* followed in 1996, its soundtrack peaking at No. 1 on the Billboard Top R&B Albums chart. The soundtrack also became the first and only gospel album in history to sell a million copies in Europe. With the release of *My Love Is Your Love* in 1998, Whitney returned to non-soundtrack material for the first time in eight years. On the album, she fully swaddled herself in R&B, as evinced by the lead single 'Heartbreak Hotel' featuring leading R&B ladies Faith Evans and Kelly Price. 'Heartbreak Hotel' peaked at No. 2 on the Hot 100 and No. 1 on the R&B chart. 'It's Not Right But It's Okay' followed, an unflinching single about infidelity that saw Whitney singing over

> We all know what a miraculous singer Whitney was – perhaps the greatest voice of our time.
>
> **ALICIA KEYS**

infectiously catchy production by Rodney 'Darkchild' Jerkins. The single reached No. 1 on the UK Hip Hop and R&B Chart and No. 1 on the US Dance Club Songs chart. At the 2000 Grammys, Whitney won the award for Best Female R&B Vocal Performance for the song, after years of being nominated (and winning) in the Pop Vocal category.

In March 2000, Whitney Houston was named Female Artist of the Decade at the Soul Train Music Awards, a 180-degree turnaround from the negative reaction she received in 1989. Her following release, 2002's *Just Whitney*, saw Houston creating without Clive Davis for the

After eight years producing soundtrack material, Whitney returned to album form with the 1998 release of the R&B-centric *My Love Is Your Love*.

first time, instead working with a host of talented hitmakers including Babyface, Missy Elliott and Kevin 'She'kspere' Briggs. In 2009, Whitney's final album, *I Look to You*, debuted at No. 1 on the Billboard 200. It reflected a mature Whitney who was returning to her gospel roots and re-establishing her connection to a higher power, as heard on the moving 'I Didn't Know My Own Strength' and the piano-driven title track, written by R. Kelly. Houston also called back to her dance music roots with the feel-good, Alicia Keys-penned single 'Million Dollar Bill'.

After a life filled with private and public struggles with drug abuse, Whitney Houston passed away on February 11, 2012. Her accomplishments remain, without hyperbole, some of the most impressive ever achieved: In 2023, *Rolling Stone* named Houston as the second greatest singer of all time, only behind her inspiration, Aretha Franklin. Whitney's legacy remains relevant contemporarily, thanks to her timeless material, but also because of devoted artists like the Norwegian DJ Kygo,

Whitney Houston

ALBUMS:

Whitney Houston (1985)
Whitney (1987)
I'm Your Baby Tonight (1990)
The Bodyguard soundtrack (1992)
The Preacher's Wife soundtrack (1996)
My Love Is Your Love (1998)
Just Whitney (2002)
I Look to You (2009)

SONGS:

'Saving All My Love for You' (1985)
'How Will I Know' (1985)
'Greatest Love of All' (1986)
'I Wanna Dance with Somebody (Who Loves Me)' (1987)
'Didn't We Almost Have It All' (1987)
'So Emotional' (1987)
'Where Do Broken Hearts Go' (1988)
'I'm Your Baby Tonight' (1990)
'All the Man That I Need' (1990)
'I Will Always Love You' (1992)
'Exhale (Shoop Shoop)' (1995)
'Heartbreak Hotel' featuring Faith Evans and Kelly Price (1998)
'It's Not Right But It's Okay' (1999)
'I Didn't Know My Own Strength' (2009)
'I Look to You' (2009)
'Million Dollar Bill' (2009)

who remixed her vocals with danceable EDM ('Higher Love'). Even more substantial is Whitney's impact on the women artists who came after her: Beyoncé, Lady Gaga, Alicia Keys, Mariah Carey, Brandy and Aaliyah have acknowledged and praised Houston for her impact on their craft. In 2020, Houston was inducted into the Rock & Roll Hall of Fame by Alicia Keys. "We all know what a miraculous singer Whitney was – perhaps the greatest voice of our time,' Keys said during the induction speech. 'We all know how her unprecedented success brought Black women into the absolute highest reaches of the music industry's pantheon. We all know her music will live forever. That music, that everlasting voice, is her final generous gift to us, and she will now be one of the brightest lights ever to shine in the Rock & Roll Hall of Fame."

Rolling Stone selected Houston, shown here in 2000, as the second greatest singer of all time – directly behind her inspiration, Aretha Franklin.

WHITNEY HOUSTON

WHITNEY HOUSTON, 'I WILL ALWAYS LOVE YOU'

Release date: November 3, 1992
Album: *The Bodyguard* soundtrack
Recorded: 1992
Label: Arista
Studio: Ocean Way Recording (Los Angeles)
Songwriter: Dolly Parton
Billboard Hot 100: 1
UK Singles Chart: 1

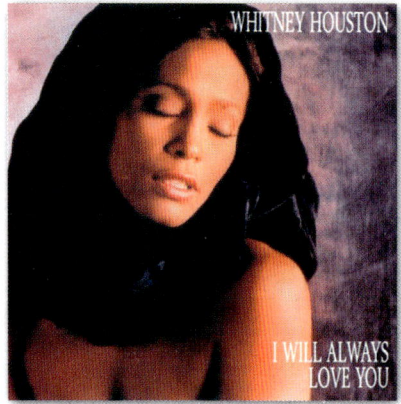

Critical Acclaim

The world-shifting lead single of *The Bodyguard* soundtrack, 'I Will Always Love You' peaked at No. 1 for a then-record breaking 14 weeks and became the biggest selling single by a female artist in history. 'I think Dolly Parton is a hell of a writer and a hell of a singer,' Whitney told *Rolling Stone*. 'I was concerned when I sang her song how she'd feel about it, in terms of the arrangement, my licks, my flavor. When she said she was floored, that meant so much to me.'

Recording

David Foster, producer of 'I Will Always Love You', initially had a different vision for the song. "Kevin Costner had said to me, 'When she sings that song in the first chorus, I want it to be with no music," Foster said in *Whitney: Can I Be Me*. "And I said, Kevin, that's so stupid. No music, are you kidding me? We're trying to get on radio? And I'm standing there and she goes, *If, I…* And it was like, Oh my

God, are you kidding me? This is the most incredible thing I've ever seen in my life. And my demo did not include that. I had music right from the start. And from that second on, I knew that the only way that record could ever be that way was with that a capella opening. It was just one of the most breathtaking things I've ever been part of, and it wasn't even my doing, it was Kevin Costner."

Legacy

Houston's version of 'I Will Always Love You' went on to win Record of the Year and Best Female Pop Vocal Performance at the 1994 Grammy Awards. Diamond-certified by the RIAA in the US, the song was also internationally beloved, topping the singles charts in at least 34 countries, including the Eurochart Hot 100 Singles, where it spent 13 weeks at the top. In 2019, the Library of Congress added Houston's version to the National Recording Registry.

Remixes

In 2000, a special collector's box set of unreleased Whitney Houston mixes was released, and the propulsive, 9 minute plus-long Hex Hector Club Mix of 'I Will Always Love You' was included.

Covers

- **2012, *Glee* cast -** Amber Riley performed the song in the episode 'Heart', and the show's producers dedicated it as a tribute to the late Houston.

MARIAH
CAREY

Mariah Carey's career is one long, verified receipt. She's one of the bestselling artists of all time, and her longevity across multiple decades is proof of her extensive catalogue of timeless material. Perhaps the most enduring diva of pop, Mariah Carey is also the most deserving of her status.

W hile she's been showered with multiple nicknames like 'Songbird Supreme' and the 'Queen of Christmas' and her own self-attributed 'Elusive Chanteuse', none of the titles come close to encapsulating who Mariah Carey is as an overall musician. Carey's performance as a top-tier vocalist with a five-octave range is informed by her sought-after, imaginative yet grounded songwriting skills and her work as a hands-on producer, all of which has been largely undiscussed. "The average person who's not a fan or doesn't follow what I do, they'll be like, 'Oh, you write songs?'" Mariah said during a live interview with *Genius* in November 2018. "They just don't know because it's not something that – I'm not seen sitting behind a piano or strumming a guitar, for the most part. I've had those moments, but that's not really what people associate me with, so I feel like I can't expect people to know. It would make me happy. It makes me extremely happy when people say a song has affected their lives, something that I've written that's come from a very personal place has affected or impacted upon somebody else in an important way."

With 19 No. 1 records under her Santa Claus belt, and 18 of those songs written or cowritten by Mariah herself (the exception is her cover of The Jackson 5's 'I'll Be There'), Carey stands only behind The Beatles for most songs atop the Billboard Hot 100. But before Mariah became one of the most awarded and exalted artists of all time, she had to overcome a difficult childhood. Born on Long Island, New York during a moment in the space-time continuum she doesn't recognize ("I don't acknowledge time," Carey told *W Magazine* in November 2022. "I don't know her"), Mariah Carey is the daughter of an Irish American mother who sang in the New York City Opera and a Black and Venezuelan father who worked in aeronautics. "My mother was disowned by her family," Carey revealed to *Interview Magazine* in October 1999. "Then my parents got divorced, which was probably very good for me. It happened when I was three. My brother and sister had a much worse childhood, I think, because they were older, and they had to deal with a lot more racism because they grew up in

the '70s and I grew up more in the '80s. So they had to deal with crosses being burned on their lawn and their dogs being poisoned."

After her parents divorced, Carey was raised by her mother, who was trained as both a jazz and classical singer and gave vocal lessons in her free time. "I didn't gravitate toward opera for my own listening pleasure or to sing," Mariah recalled in an interview with *Music Connection* in February 1991. "But it was around me, and I would hear [my mother] singing all of the time. She also sang jazz. She was listening to a lot of Sarah Vaughan, Billie Holiday, Ella Fitzgerald, and I had those influences as well." In addition to jazz pioneers, Mariah was obsessed with R&B idols like Aretha Franklin and gospel greats like Shirley Caesar. "She had to drag me away from the radio when I was a little girl and make me go to bed because I was just singing constantly," Mariah said.

Known for her five-octave vocal range, Carey's true artistry lies in her severely overlooked roles as a gifted songwriter and producer.

By the time she reached high school, Carey was determined to make it in the music industry as a professional singer-songwriter. She had a God-given knack for crafting melodies and lyrics and she knew the vision she had for herself as a trained vocalist under her mother's tutelage; even so, Mariah found herself facing an uphill battle with the collaborative creative process. "It's always been a struggle," Mariah told *Pitchfork* in November 2018. 'Even when I first started making my first demos, and there was no record deal yet. I would be like, 'Can you take the strings out here,' or 'Can you make the drums break down here?' When you're a teenage girl working with what seemed like older people – who were like 25 or 30 – and it was their studio, they are the authority figures. I was producing but I didn't realize that that was producing."

As a teenager, Carey began singing backup for freestyle singer Brenda K. Starr, who invited Mariah to attend a Columbia Records party in 1988. Carey handed her demo tape to the head of the label (and her eventual first husband) Tommy Mottola, who signed her to Columbia as soon as he possibly could. Carey worked on her debut with producers Narada Michael Walden, Ric Wake and Rhett Lawrence, the latter of whom spent a considerable amount of time with Carey in the studio. "One time while Pat Dillett [the engineer who worked with Carey in New York] and I were doing background vocals, I asked Mariah to double the melody," Lawrence recalled to *Music Connection*.

> **It makes me extremely happy when people say a song has affected their lives.**
>
> **MARIAH CAREY**

"And so she doubled the melody – no problem. And then I said, 'Okay, double it an octave up.' And she doubled it an octave up. I smiled at Pat, and we started playing a game with her. So I said, 'Go ahead and double it an octave above that.' And she did it with no problem – she just kind of smiled. [Pat and I] just looked at each other. It was amazing, because it was a pretty complicated riff, and it just sounded perfect. So, I asked her if she could double it an octave above that. And she did it – no problem. We were floored! To be able to work with somebody [who] can do just about anything that you can think of vocally is a real pleasure."

As a young producer with extraordinary vocal abilities, Carey stunned industry veterans early on.

Mariah's self-titled debut was released in 1990 and preceded by the massively successful lead single 'Vision of Love', which introduced the world to her honeyed voice and deft songwriting skills. "What I do a lot of the time is, I'll write something that may seem like it is a love song or whatever, but really it's about other things," Mariah told *Music Connection*. "For example, 'Vision of Love' isn't really about a guy-girl love relationship. It's more like a celebration. In my life, I was going through a major turning point – I was going through my deal, which was a big accomplishment for me. I was really happy and things were starting to go great for me. It's really about realizing dreams and, sure, there's a little bit about a love situation, too."

The single introduced Mariah Carey as a melismatic vocalist with exceptional range, including her ability to sing effortlessly in the whistle register. 'Vision of Love' topped the singles charts in Canada, New Zealand and the US, where it reached the top of the Hot R&B/Hip-Hop Songs chart and spent four weeks at No. 1 on the Hot 100. The song was nominated for the main categories of Record of the Year and Song of the Year at the 1991 Grammy Awards and won for Best Female Pop Vocal Performance. The following three singles, 'Love Takes Time', 'Someday', and 'I Don't Wanna Cry', also reached No. 1 in the US, making Carey the first artist since The Jackson 5 to have their first four singles reach the top of the charts. In its 36th week on the Billboard 200, *Mariah Carey* topped the chart and stayed there for 11 consecutive weeks; it has since been certified nine times platinum.

Her follow-up album, 1991's *Emotions*, was inspired by the rhythm and blues of the late '60s and early '80s. "There's a rawness about those periods in R&B that's somewhat lacking today," Mariah said in a September 1991 interview with *New York Magazine*. "*Emotions* has a little bit of an older-type vibe, a Motown feel. The music I like is vocally driven." The title track hit No. 1, thanks to its upbeat production and Mariah's far-reaching vocal acrobatics, but the album itself failed to attain the same

levels of success as her debut. Even with the threat of a sophomore slump looming over her head, Mariah was certain that she could still remain in the industry and be successful. "If I wanted to stay home and write songs and make a moderate living, I could do that," Carey told *New York Magazine*. "I'm not worried that I have to go back and waitress."

Music Box, her 1993 release, all but confirmed that Mariah Carey would never have to waitress again. The lead single, 'Dreamlover', prominently featured sampling from 'Blind Alley' by The Emotions – previously used in Big Daddy Kane's 1988 single 'Ain't No Half-Steppin''. After being introduced as a pop ballad belter on her debut, then turning toward

Carey's self-titled 1990 debut introduced her as a blossoming powerhouse diva and gifted songwriter, highlighted by her chart-topping single 'Vision of Love.'

gospel-soul for *Emotions*, Mariah made a marked shift into the hip-hop world with 'Dreamlover'. To underscore this effort, Carey worked with Dave Hall, who had previously produced Mary J. Blige's 1992 album *What's the 411?* 'Dreamlover' was a global success, sitting atop the Hot 100 for eight straight weeks. It also peaked at No. 1 in Canada and Panama and was a top 10 hit in the UK, Australia, the Netherlands, New Zealand and Portugal.

'Hero', the second single from *Music Box*, became one of Carey's biggest hits – and she didn't initially write it for herself. "After I wrote 'Hero' for a while I was like, Ugh, this song is so schmaltzy, I can't take it anymore,'" Carey told *Pitchfork*. "Tommy [Mottola] had said, 'Oh, there's this movie, and Luther [Vandross] is gonna do a song, and Gloria [Estefan] is gonna do a song. You want to write the song for Gloria?' I said, 'Cool,' and then I walked out, went to the restroom, came back, and I came up with the melody and the lyric – [sings] *and then a hero comes along* – at the same

Carey's global success reached new heights with the release of 'All I Want for Christmas Is You,' the best-selling holiday song in US history.

time. I think I wouldn't have written that song for myself." Deemed by many as Mariah's signature song, 'Hero' was another worldwide success, reaching the top 10 in Australia and the UK, the top five in Canada, France, Ireland, New Zealand and Norway, and No. 1 on the Hot 100.

In 1994, Mariah Carey released what would become a career-altering album: *Merry Christmas*. Brimming with holiday standards such as 'Silent Night' and 'Joy to the World', the collection also featured the instantaneous Christmas classic, 'All I Want for Christmas Is You', which Mariah dreamed up herself after a nudge from her label. "The idea of me doing a Christmas album at all came from the record company," Mariah told *W Magazine*. "It was very early in my career, and I thought it was a little early for me to be doing that, but I was like, 'Well, I love Christmas.' I had some very sad Christmases as a child, but I always try to find the bright light there. I was sort of up late, walking around this house where I was living with my

> 66 **[The studio is] such a safe place for me and the right environment.**
> **MARIAH CAREY**

first ex-husband [Tommy Mottola], and I had a keyboard, and, no, I am by no means a piano player, but I can pluck out chords when I need to … I didn't want it to feel specific to any era, so we didn't use sounds that were happening at that time. That way, it would feel classic and timeless. But I could never have imagined that it would become such a major part of my life." 'All I Want for Christmas Is You' has officially charted every holiday season since it was released, often hitting No. 1. In fact, it has broken the record for the longest gap between release and reaching No. 1 in both the US and the UK. It remains the bestselling Christmas song of all time in the US at 16 times platinum, and is also certified diamond in Australia, Canada and Sweden. In 2023, the song was selected by the Library of Congress to be included in the National Recording Registry.

A string of hits followed from 1995's *Daydream*, including 'Fantasy', which would receive a remix featuring the Wu-Tang Clan's Ol' Dirty Bastard that her label didn't quite understand. "Those remixes were the only things I did during that time where there wasn't somebody coming in trying to control things or pretending that they knew what my music should be like," Carey told *W Magazine*. During her conversation with *Genius*, Carey elaborated on the knee-jerk reaction from Columbia. "They were like, 'What is she doing?'" she recalled. "They really didn't understand and it just became a thing. Certain people were like, 'I could do that. What is that? What is he doing?' And I'm like, 'No, no, no, no, no, just trust me, we're good.'" 'Fantasy' debuted atop the Hot 100 chart, the first single by a female artist to do so, and only the second single ever to do so after Michael Jackson's 'You Are Not Alone'. 'One Sweet Day', a collaboration with Boyz II Men, topped the Hot 100 for 16 straight weeks, becoming the longest-running No. 1 song in the chart's history, a record held for 23 years.

The late '90s represented Mariah's breakaway from her eventual ex-husband and the label he ran (Sony/Columbia). She continued to shift further into the hip-hop space with 1997's *Butterfly* and 1999's *Rainbow*, collaborating with Bad Boy and The Lox ('Honey'), Mobb Deep ('The Roof [Back In Time]'), Bone Thugs-N-Harmony ('Breakdown') and Jay-Z

Carey pioneered the hip-hop/pop crossover dynamic with hits like 'Fantasy' and 'Honey.'

('Heartbreaker'). All the while, Carey continued to deliver the thrilling, heartfelt balladry and soaring high notes that she first became known for ('Butterfly', 'Can't Take That Away [Mariah's Theme]'). In 2001, Mariah hit a rough patch with the release of the *Glitter* film and soundtrack. "*Glitter* was, people looked at it like, 'Oh, that's her downfall, that's it,'" Mariah said at *Genius*. "So then I signed with Universal. [CEO] Doug Morris and I had this incredible meeting and he was like, 'I believe in you,' such this and such. We did the *Charmbracelet* album, but I think had they released different songs from that album, it would have done better. But everybody was like, 'Oh, let's have a sob story, let's release 'Through the Rain'.' I wrote it. I'm not hating on my own song – a little bit, maybe. I don't mean to. With that album, it was like there *was* something to prove. And then we didn't really prove it because it wasn't a big hit."

The Emancipation of Mimi, released in 2005, was *the* hit Carey had been hoping for, and it was Mariah's first album on Island Records, which eventually merged with Def Jam. Highlighted by songs like 'It's Like That' with Jermaine Dupri (whom she worked with on the 1996 hit single 'Always Be My Baby') and 'Shake It Off', the biggest single of the album was 'We Belong Together', a career redefining single that topped the Hot 100 for 14 non-consecutive weeks, at that point in rare company, including Carey's own Boyz II Men collaboration 'One Sweet Day'. *Billboard* declared it the 'song of the decade' and it broke several airplay records, garnering both the largest one-day and one-week audiences in history. 'We Belong Together' also reached the top five in more than ten countries, including the UK, Ireland, the Netherlands, New Zealand and Spain.

Mariah absorbed the reaction to *Emancipation* and continued on her journey of melding the worlds of hip-hop and R&B with adult contemporary on her following albums: 2008's *E=MC²* ('Touch My Body'), 2009's *Memoirs of an Imperfect Angel* ('Obsessed') and 2014's *Me. I Am Mariah... The Elusive Chanteuse* ('#Beautiful' with Miguel). In 2018, she released *Caution*, which was led by the deceptively simple breakup song 'GTFO'. The album itself represented Mariah's freedom and desire to create from a place of authenticity. "Really, it was just getting back in the studio," Carey told *Genius*. "It's such a safe place for me and the right environment. I had been outside of that environment for too long and doing too many superfluous things that I really didn't need to be doing. And I was just so happy to be back in the studio and I really wanted to collaborate. Occasionally, or sometimes, the thing is like, 'Let me sit alone and really wrack my brain and write these lyrics because I need to express that as a full vision.' But then, one of my favorite things to do is collaborate and go back and forth. Sit here with you and be like,

Mariah Carey

ALBUMS:

Mariah Carey (1990)
Emotions (1991)
Music Box (1993)
Merry Christmas (1994)
Daydream (1995)
Butterfly (1997)
Rainbow (1999)
Glitter (2001)
Charmbracelet (2002)
The Emancipation of Mimi (2005)
E=MC² (2008)
Memoirs of an Imperfect Angel (2009)
Me. I Am Mariah… The Elusive Chanteuse (2014)
Caution (2018)

SONGS:

'Vision of Love' (1990)
'Love Takes Time' (1990)
'Someday' (1991)
'I Don't Wanna Cry' (1991)
'Emotions' (1991)
'Dreamlover' (1993)
'Hero' (1993)
'All I Want for Christmas Is You' (1994)
'Fantasy' (1995)
'One Sweet Day' with Boyz II Men (1995)
'Always Be My Baby' (1996)
'Honey' (1997)
'Butterfly' (1997)
'The Roof (Back In Time)' (1998)
'Breakdown' (1998)
'Heartbreaker' (1999)
'Can't Take That Away (Mariah's Theme)' (2000)
'It's Like That' (2005)
'We Belong Together' (2005)
'Shake It Off' (2005)
'Touch My Body' (2008)
'Obsessed' (2009)
'#Beautiful' (2013)
'GTFO' (2018)

'How about this? How about that?' Really have a dialogue about it and then come up with an end result. I did a lot of that on this record."

Viewing Mariah Carey as a simple pop diva is a restricted perspective. Her status as an undeniable hitmaker extends across genres, from pop to dance to hip-hop to R&B. Mariah continues to inspire her successors, including artists like Atlanta MC Latto, who sampled 'Fantasy' for her 2021 single 'Big Energy' and included re-recorded vocals from Mariah on the remix. In 2022, Carey was inducted into the Songwriters Hall of Fame, a long overdue recognition. "I just want to say, my whole journey started with poetry, in my childhood," Carey said during her speech. "And then – well, actually, I believe melodies came first. And then I started writing these poems, and people were like, 'This girl has kind of a dark vision of the world at six years old.' And I did, because I came from this incredibly dysfunctional background. And it was this whole thing, music, and walking by myself and coming up with melodies and writing words in a book … Out of the 439 total inductees into the Songwriters Hall of Fame, only 32 have been women up until this moment. Now it's 33. As my father once told me: 'You did good, kid.'"

In 2022, Carey was finally inducted into the Songwriters Hall of Fame, affirming her legacy as a masterful songwriter and boundary-pushing artist.

MARIAH CAREY, 'WE BELONG TOGETHER'

Release date: March 15, 2005
Album: *The Emancipation of Mimi*
Recorded: 2004
Label: Island Def Jam
Studio: Right Track (New York City); Southside (Atlanta)
Songwriters: Mariah Carey, Kenneth 'Babyface' Edmonds, Bobby Womack, Darnell Bristol, Jermaine Dupri, Johnta Austin, Manuel Seal, Patrick Moten, Sandra E. Sully, Sid Johnson
Billboard Hot 100: 1
UK Singles Chart: 2

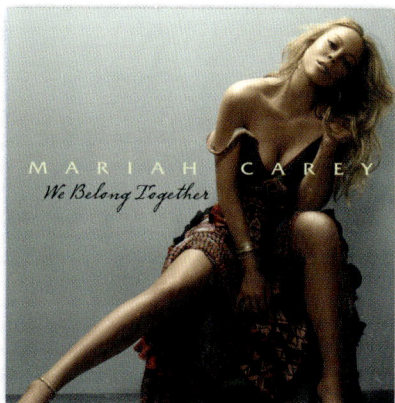

Critical Acclaim

In 2001, Mariah hit a rough patch with the release of the *Glitter* film and soundtrack. "Glitter was, people looked at it like, Oh, that's her downfall, that's it," Mariah recalled during a career-spanning conversation at *Genius*. "So then I signed with Universal. [CEO] Doug Morris and I had this incredible meeting and he was like, I believe in you, such this and such. We did the *Charmbracelet* album … With that album, it was like there was something to prove. And then we didn't really prove it because it wasn't a big hit." *The Emancipation of Mimi*, released in 2005, was the comeback hit Carey had been hoping for. The biggest single of the album was 'We Belong Together', a career re-defining song that topped the Hot 100 for 14 non-consecutive weeks.

Recording

'We Belong Together' was written by Carey, Jermaine Dupri, Manuel Seal, and Johntá Austin, and produced by Carey and Dupri. Built on a coaxing piano arrangement with a compelling backbeat, the song features lyrics that tell the story of a woman desperately trying to convince her lover to return. Carey interpolates lyrics from Bobby Womack's 'If You Think You're Lonely Now' and The Deele's 'Two Occasions,' so the songwriters of those songs are credited respectively.

Legacy

'We Belong Together' was Carey's 16th chart-topper on the Hot 100. *Billboard* declared it the 'song of the decade' and it broke several airplay records, garnering both the largest one-day and one-week audiences in history. 'We Belong Together' also reached the top five in more than ten countries, including the UK, Ireland, the Netherlands, New Zealand and Spain. The song went on to win the 2006 Grammy Awards for Best Female R&B Vocal Performance and Best R&B Song.

Remixes

The official 'We Belong Together' remix featured Jadakiss and Styles P, with hard-hitting production handled by DJ Clue and Carey. In 2021, Mariah released a version subtitled 'Mimi's Late Night Valentine,' an extended, seven-minute mix of the song that featured live instrumentation.

Covers

- **2020, Ni/Co -** The Los Angeles-based pop group performed a live version that has reached nearly 5 million views on YouTube.
- **2025, Sheer Element -** The pair of R&B vocalists covered the song on TikTok, amassing over 5 million views, which led to an extended live version on YouTube.

MARY J.
BLIGE

Upon the release of her debut 1992 album *What's the 411?* Mary J. Blige was christened the Queen of Hip-Hop Soul. More than three decades later, she has unwaveringly retained that title. Blige's dogged tenacity has carried her throughout her extensive career, which has been marked time and again by her willingness to lay bare her life's most challenging moments.

Blige's autobiographical, honesty-soaked approach has coloured her entire discography but her biggest hit to date, 2001's 'Family Affair', offered her an escape from the pain she endured throughout her life at the hands of others, in addition to her own self-inflicted wounds. Produced by Dr. Dre, 'Family Affair' was written by Blige, her brother Bruce Miller and Dr. Dre's frequent collaborators Camara Kambon (who composed the theme song for the Black female-led sitcom *Girlfriends*) and Michael Elizondo (known for cowriting 'In da Club' by 50 Cent and 'The Real Slim Shady' by Eminem). A celebratory song, 'Family Affair' relies equally

The celebratory 'Family Affair' was Blige's biggest hit, but it was an outlier from the singer's raw, autobiographically honest discography.

on Dr. Dre's uptempo, post-G-Funk production and Blige's punchy delivery of lyrics.

The song's encouragement to bask in an unabashed lust for life connected with audiences: 'Family Affair' reached No. 1 on Billboard's Hot 100 chart and remained there for six weeks. It also reached No. 1 in France and No. 2 on the UK Hip Hop and R&B chart. Even though it was the runaway hit single from Blige's 2001 album *No More Drama*, the artist found herself trapped in the self-destructive habits that she had developed as a young girl. "After *No More Drama*, I had the biggest record in the country, but I didn't feel it," she told Oprah Winfrey in a May 2006 issue of *O* magazine. "I was slowly killing myself, drink after drink."

Born Mary Jane Blige in 1971 in the Bronx, New York, the singer-songwriter spent her early years in Richmond Hill, Georgia. It wasn't long before she and her family moved back to Yonkers, New York, living in the rough Schlobohm Housing Projects. Blige's father, an abusive alcoholic Vietnam War veteran, left the home when she was four years old. The following year, Blige was sexually abused by a family friend who was entrusted to be her caretaker. From that moment forward, Blige faced major difficulties with vocalizing her personal issues and maintaining a sense of self-worth. "That thing followed me all my life," she confessed on VH1's *Behind the Music*. "The shame of thinking my molestation was my fault – it led me to believe I wasn't worth anything."

As a young teen, she found solace in alcohol and drugs and became promiscuous as a means of controlling her own life and sexuality. "I ended up becoming my environment," she told *Parade* magazine in 2007. "It was bigger than me. I had no self-respect. I hated myself. I thought I was ugly. Alcohol, sex, drugs – I'd do whatever it took to feel better."

Blige dropped out of high school during her junior year, but her love for music kept her motivated. Her experiences singing in church throughout her adolescence stuck with her and in 1988, at age 17, Blige did something that would change her life: She sang Anita Baker's 'Caught Up in the Rapture' in a karaoke booth at a mall in White Plains, New York. The resulting tape found its way to Uptown Records CEO Andre Harrell, who was so intrigued by Mary's innate vocal abilities that he visited her at her family's small project apartment. He heard the raw, yet talented, Blige sing and immediately signed her to his label.

Early on, Mary J. Blige sang backup for other acts on the label, like Father MC; Blige's vocals can be heard on the rapper's biggest hit, 1990's 'I'll Do 4 U'. Shortly after, Blige began working with Harrell's protege, Sean 'Puffy' Combs, on her 1992 debut album, *What's the 411?* Guided by Harrell's "ghetto fabulous" ethos – embracing the oft-negated yet authentic elements of Black culture, instead of shying away from them – Blige and Combs brought forth a brand-new sound.

While the flavour of New Jack Swing was still in the air, Blige's project introduced the world to a sister subgenre: hip-hop soul. By combining hard-hitting rap beats with a swirl of undeniably soulful vocals, *What's the 411?* represented a shift in the sonic landscape. "I wasn't conscious that I was doing something different in that moment," Blige told NPR in April 2017. "I just knew that I loved hip-hop and R&B, and I was doing what I loved. And I didn't realize what we had done 'til later, like, 'Wow, we created a whole genre of music.'"

In addition to a fresh sound, Blige also brought with her a multitude of experiences from her past. 'You Remind Me', the album's lead single, had flecks of New Jack Swing and saw Blige singing passionately about a reminiscent love. The song hit No. 1 on the Billboard R&B chart and reached No. 29 on the Hot 100. It was also featured on the 1991 comedy film soundtrack *Strictly Business*. The follow-up single, 'Real Love', borrowed its instantly recognizable drums from the

> I didn't realize what we had done 'til later, like, 'Wow, we created a whole genre of music.'
>
> **MARY J. BLIGE**

1987, now hip-hop classic, 'Top Billin'' by Audio Two. On top of the head-nodding percussive elements, 'Real Love' is buoyed by Blige's yearning vocals, as she croons about her desire for a romance that surpasses her expectations. 'Real Love' had major success for Blige, as it broke into the top 10 of the Billboard Hot 100, at slot No. 7, demonstrating the relatability of the song.

Mary J. Blige's ability to tap into her innermost longings and passions would lend itself well to her sophomore album, 1994's *My Life*. By this

Blige's life changed at age 17, when a karaoke tape led to a record deal and her pioneering, hip-hop soul debut *What's the 411?*

point, Blige was deep into an abusive relationship with K-Ci Hailey of Jodeci and she was coping with her old vices from her youth. Those experiences bled through on *My Life*. "It is a lot of pain in it, but it's pain now that's translated into joy," Blige told *Billboard* in June 2021. "We're living to tell this story. There's a time that I didn't want to live. I hated myself. I didn't think anything of myself. But the beauty is that I lived to tell the story, and now I don't hate myself. I've developed some love for myself. And it's helped so many people, and they're living to tell the story."

"I was in a state of mind where I didn't wanna live," Blige explained further in an August 2024 *HuffPost* interview. "I was on drugs. I was going through hell. I was in abusive relationship after abusive relationship. I just completely hated myself. There was something that happened where I had to choose life during that time as much as I wanted to kill myself, and I didn't wanna take 400 people with me because the Mary J. Blige fan base was die-hard." Through songs like the title track, which deftly samples 'Everybody Loves the Sunshine' by Roy Ayers Ubiquity, and 'Be Happy,' which borrows liberally from 'You're So Good to Me' by Curtis Mayfield, Blige continued to tap into her vulnerable side. By confronting and releasing the emotions that raged like a storm within her, Blige gave listeners permission to do the same.

In 1995, Blige expanded artistically, working with Method Man on a cover of Marvin Gaye and Tammi Terrell's 'I'll Be There for You/ You're All I Need to Get By', a hauntingly beautiful duet that explored a contemporary take on a committed relationship. Blige would go on to win her first Grammy Award for the song in 1996, for Best Rap Performance by a Duo or Group. That same year, she was featured on an ambitious newcomer's breakthrough single, Jay-Z's 'Can't Knock

Blige channeled her deepest pain from addiction and abuse and transformed it into vulnerable, soulful music that resonated with her fans on a personal level.

the Hustle'. Her raspy, assuring voice accentuated the success-by-any-means-necessary messaging of the song. The Babyface written and produced 'Not Gon' Cry' was initially sung by Blige for the popular soundtrack of the 1995 film *Waiting to Exhale* and would later appear on her 1997 album *Share My World*. Overflowing with emotion, the Grammy-nominated song showcased a resilient Blige, who took on the lyrics of betrayal as if she lived them herself. Also on *Share My World* is the unflinching 'I Can Love You' featuring a fiery verse from Lil' Kim, the Nas-assisted, Rick James 'Moonchild' sampling 'Love Is All We Need' and the resigned 'Seven Days', which saw Blige collaborating with jazz fusion musician George Benson.

With the release of her follow-up albums, 1998's *Mary*, 2001's *No More Drama* and 2002's *Love & Life*, Mary J. Blige continued to turn out major hits ('Family Affair', 'No More Drama', 'All That I Can Say'

Blige's journey from suffering to empowerment was reflected in her ever-expanding music as she navigated love, fame and personal growth through albums like 2005's *The Breakthrough*.

with Ms. Lauryn Hill). It was her 2005 album *The Breakthrough* that saw Blige turning a corner and striding away from the pain that had carried her for so long throughout her career. At this point, Blige had met a new partner Kendu Isaacs, who doubled as her manager. She felt as though she had been given a new lease on life and love.

The standout lead single, 'Be Without You', was written by Johntá Austin, Bryan-Michael Cox, Jason Perry and Blige herself. A piano-laden ode to her newfound love, the song reached No. 3 on the Billboard Hot 100 and No. 1 on the R&B chart. In 2017, *Billboard* ranked the song as the most successful R&B/hip-hop song of all time. *The Breakthrough* was nominated for eight Grammy Awards and won three: Best R&B album, Best R&B Song and Best R&B Female Vocal Performance for 'Be Without You'. But with the change in material

In my case, I'm not going to be broken.
MARY J. BLIGE

came a visceral reaction from fans. "A lot of people hate me for this," Blige told Oprah Winfrey. "People say things like, 'Mary, I liked it better when you were singing them sad songs. You need to pick up a pack of cigarettes and come back down with us.' It blows my mind – then again, not really. They just want someone to [wallow] with them in their environment."

The 2007 album *Growing Pains* featured a Mary J. Blige who was committed to sharing her new outlook on life. 'Just Fine', an encouraging, celebratory anthem, was unlike anything her fans had heard before – and they embraced it. In 2016, Blige divorced from Isaacs and had to find herself again. From that moment forward, the megastar has been focused on transcending the expectations that have been placed upon her. After years of onscreen work, Blige was nominated for two Academy Awards in 2017, for her supporting role in the film

Mary J. Blige

ALBUMS:

What's the 411? (1992)
My Life (1994)
Share My World (1997)
Mary (1999)
No More Drama (2001)
Love & Life (2003)
The Breakthrough (2005)
Growing Pains (2007)
Stronger with Each Tear (2009)
My Life II... The Journey Continues (Act 1) (2011)
The London Sessions (2014)
Strength of a Woman (2017)
Good Morning Gorgeous (2022)
Gratitude (2024)

SONGS:

'You Remind Me' (1992)
'Real Love' (1992)
'I'm Goin' Down' (1995)
'I'll Be There for You/You're All I Need to Get By' with Method Man (1995)
'Not Gon' Cry' (1996)
'I Can Love You' featuring Lil' Kim (1997)
'Love Is All We Need' (1997)
'Everything' (1997)
'Seven Days' (1998)
'All That I Can Say' (1999)
'Family Affair' (2001)
'No More Drama' (2001)
'Be Without You' (2005)
'Just Fine' (2007)
'Mighty River' (2017)
'Need You More' featuring Jadakiss (2024)
'Breathing' featuring Fabolous (2024)
'I Got Plans' featuring A$AP Ferg (2024)

Mudbound and for the original song 'Mighty River', becoming the first person to be nominated for acting and songwriting in the same year.

In addition to 2022's *Good Morning Gorgeous*, Blige's 2024 album *Gratitude* represented her moment to reintroduce herself as a veteran artist. She circled back to her roots of hip-hop soul, working with former rap collaborators like Jadakiss ('Need You More') and Fabolous ('Breathing'), as well as newer acts like A$AP Ferg ('I Got Plans').

Blige has said herself that she doesn't plan to make music forever, mentioning in 2024 that she could foresee an impending retirement within five to six years. After being inducted into the Rock & Roll Hall of Fame in 2024, the artist has little left to prove – but that doesn't mean she's done overcoming yet. "I'm building for expansion, I'm building for longevity, I'm building for legacy, and I'm building for history," she said during her induction speech, flanked by Dr. Dre and Method Man, two of her more successful collaborative colleagues. "This whole time, I was building to be a rock star and now I am. The Queen of Hip-Hop Soul is a rock star."

Through every peak and valley of her life, Mary J. Blige has never shied away from sharing her reasons for pushing through. From the devastating to the delightful, her music has made it clear that she's more than a victim of her circumstances – she's a survivor who has helped countless others to make it another day. "It's hard," she told NPR. "It's a responsibility being Mary J. Blige. I wouldn't trade it, but the trials and tribulations I could do without. If I could do it without the trials – but those are the things that make us or break us. And, in my case, I'm not going to be broken."

In 2017, Blige became the first person to be nominated for acting (for her supporting role in the film *Mudbound*) and songwriting (for the original song 'Mighty River') in the same year at the Academy Awards.

MARY J. BLIGE, 'FAMILY AFFAIR'

Release date: July 2001
Album: *No More Drama*
Recorded: 2000–2001
Label: MCA
Studio: Record One (Sherman Oaks, California); Quad Recording Studios (Manhattan)
Songwriters: Mary J. Blige, Bruce Miller, Andre 'Dr. Dre' Young, Camara Kambon, Michael Elizondo
Billboard Hot 100: 1
UK Singles Chart: 8

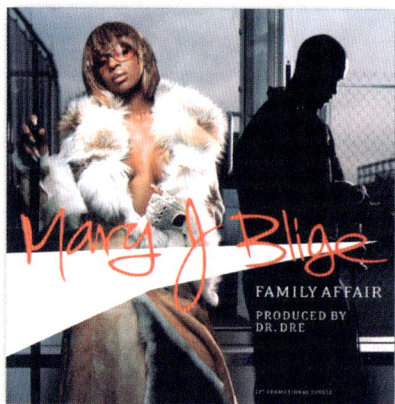

Critical Acclaim

Blige's autobiographical, honesty-soaked approach has coloured her entire discography but her biggest hit to date, 2001's 'Family Affair', offered her an escape from the pain she endured throughout her life at the hands of others, in addition to her own self-inflicted wounds.

Recording

Produced by Dr. Dre, 'Family Affair' was written by Blige, her brother Bruce Miller and Dr. Dre's frequent collaborators Camara Kambon and Michael Elizondo. A celebratory song, 'Family Affair' relies equally on Dr. Dre's uptempo, post-G-Funk production and Mary J. Blige's punchy lyrical delivery.

Legacy

The song's encouragement to bask in an unabashed lust for life connected with audiences: 'Family Affair' held the No. 1 spot on *Billboard*'s Hot 100 chart for six weeks. It also reached No. 1 in France and No. 2 on the UK hip-hop/R&B chart.

Remixes

The official 'Family Affair' remix featured Jadakiss and Fabolous, and maintained Dr. Dre's production. The trailblazing hip-hop group Pete Rock & C.L. Smooth released a laidback remix of their own, while the UK duo Sharp Boys offered up a high-energy dance rendition. French megaproducer David Guetta also remixed the song, turning it into a heart-pumping event.

Covers

- **2019, Eagles of Death Metal** - Jesse 'Boots Electric' Hughes, the frontman of the California rock band, recorded his own version of the song on the album *Eagles Of Death Metal Presents Boots Electric Performing The Best Songs We Never Wrote*.

AALIYAH

Though her life was tragically cut short at 22 years old, Aaliyah had an outsized impact on R&B in a condensed amount of time. Eventually becoming known as the "Princess of R&B," she knew early on that she wanted to influence the music industry, and the world at large, using her music as a vessel. Through her singing, acting, dancing and modelling, Aaliyah did just that.

"It's amazing to me when I think back and think about everything that I've done and how I started at such a young age," Aaliyah said in a July 2001 interview with *Plus vite que la musique*. "I feel very blessed, I learned a lot. I've been doing this for seven years now, so I totally feel like a veteran even though I'm still very young. It's really amazing. I'm happy. I'm doing what I've always wanted to do. This is what I dreamed about doing when I was a little girl – and I'm doing it."

Born in Brooklyn in 1979, Aaliyah Dana Haughton was raised in Detroit, Michigan, along with her older brother Rashad, who would come to be involved in his sister's music and film presence. Aaliyah's mother Diane was a homemaker who dabbled in singing and her father Michael was a warehouse worker who later became her manager. Aaliyah's passion was demonstrably present since the age of six; at that time, Aaliyah was cast in an elementary school production of the stage play *Annie*, a pivotal moment that would go on to affect her immediate and future life. Aaliyah's uncle, Barry Hankerson, was married to soul star Gladys Knight in the mid-to-late '70s and co-founded his own record label, Blackground, in the early '90s.

At age 10, Aaliyah competed on the talent programme *Star Search*, performing the jazz standard 'My Funny Valentine' as a ballad. Ultimately losing, Aaliyah was determined to make the most of the experiences she had had thus far. By age 11, Aaliyah she'd been invited to perform with Gladys Knight during a stretch of five shows in Las Vegas. "I had done a lot of performances at that point and I felt it would be a really, really great learning experience," Aaliyah told *Plus vite que la musique*. "So, we went out to Las Vegas and I sang 'Home' [from *The Wiz*] in the middle of her show – she brought me out. And then she came out with me and we sang 'Believe In Yourself' together. She taught me a lot: she taught me how to work a stage, how to captivate an audience, to put emotion into a song and to not be shook by being on stage."

After signing a distribution deal with Jive Records, Hankerson signed his niece to Blackground at age 12. As the then-manager of R. Kelly, Hankerson involved the singer-songwriter and musician with moulding Aaliyah's early sound and image, which centred on mature topics and optics. Kelly quickly began writing and producing songs for Aaliyah's debut album, 1994's *Age Ain't Nothing But A Number*, invoking streetwise topics and musical elements that teetered between New Jack Swing, R&B and pop.

The rambunctious debut single 'Back & Forth' peaked at No. 5 on the Billboard Hot 100 and topped the Hot R&B/Hip-Hop Songs chart, introducing a mature-beyond-her-years young singer whose style and demeanour invited ample conversation. At the other end of the spectrum, Aaliyah covered The Isley Brothers' 1976 song 'At Your Best (You Are Love)', a true-to-form, ethereal showcasing. This song managed to score a No. 6 position on the Hot 100 and No. 2 on the Hot R&B/Hip-Hop Songs chart. Her versatility on full display, *Age Ain't Nothing But A Number* represented a first glance at Aaliyah's burgeoning talent, eventually earning a double platinum certification from the RIAA. "Coming out so young at 15 and having success at that age, of course there were times when I felt like I was in a daze and I couldn't believe that this was happening," Aaliyah told *Plus vite que la musique*. "I worked so hard; been rejected. I lost on *Star Search*. I auditioned with a lot

Aaliyah began performing as a child and learned from mentors like Gladys Knight at a young age.

of record companies that didn't think I had it. So, to finally have that album, to have that success, I was like 'Wow, I did it.'"

After rumours began swirling of Aaliyah's secret, underage marriage to R. Kelly, the singer left Jive Records and released her follow-up album on Atlantic in 1996, *One In A Million,* working closely with producer Timbaland and singer-songwriter/producer Missy Elliott. "I think that it may slip people's minds once in a while that I am just 17," Aaliyah said in 1996 on the UK music show *What's the 411.* "I consider myself still to be a baby, I'm still my mama's baby. I'm just a baby girl, that's my nickname: Baby Girl. And I feel I am. And I will always be a baby, but I think people do forget that sometimes. I'm in a business where I'm around adults on a daily basis. But you know, it comes with the territory. You have to grow up when you get in this, you gotta grow up quickly."

Aaliyah's collaborative partnership with Timbaland and Missy transformed Aaliyah's sound from New Jack Swing-inflected street R&B to a futuristic, forward-thinking sonic atmosphere that built on unconventional sounds and skittering, pitter-pattering drums. "Me and Timbaland were trying to get started, and we brought some tracks to [Aaliyah], and she loved them," Missy Elliott told *Entertainment Weekly* in December 2002. "We wound up doing eight tracks on her album. She was sincerely sweet. Me and Timb were unknown producers then and Aaliyah was a platinum artist. We thought she'd be some sort of uppity mega superstar, but when we met her, she treated us as if we were Timbaland and Missy today, as though we had a name. She made us feel like family – very warm."

The lead single, 'If Your Girl Only Knew', a contemporary, funky track chastising a cheating man, reached No. 11 on the Hot 100 and topped the Hot R&B/Hip-Hop Songs chart. The title song was, in and of itself, a distinct redirection of her previous artistic approach, with stuttering, idiosyncratic production from Timbaland and backing vocals and significant lyrical input from Missy Elliott. '4 Page Letter' followed, a contemplative, almost haunting single that saw Aaliyah expressing her feelings for her crush in a very intentional way. The succeeding single, 'The One I Gave My Heart To', was written by the prolific Diane Warren and produced by Daryl Simmons, who often worked with Babyface and

"We thought [Aaliyah would] be some sort of uppity mega superstar, but [...] she made us feel like family," Missy Elliott recounted in 2002.

L.A. Reid; it peaked at No. 9 on the Hot 100 and No. 8 on the Hot R&B/ Hip-Hop Songs chart. *One In A Million* went on to earn double platinum status, with the title track securing a gold certification.

Kathy Iandoli, author of the 2021 biography *Baby Girl: Better Known as Aaliyah*, observed the artist's transition from shielded to spotlight in a conversation with *The Independent* in July 2021. "With her debut, she was hiding in this very big shadow of R. Kelly's, where her identity on the project was dictated by his own twisted idea of what her image and sound should be," Iandoli said. "With the second album, we saw her inching into her own person, thanks to Timbaland and Missy kind of guiding her in this direction where they threw caution to the wind … But by her eponymous third project, we saw Aaliyah in her full form."

> ## You have to grow up when you get in this [industry], you gotta grow up quickly.
> **AALIYAH**

Before *Aaliyah* arrived, the singer contributed to the soundtrack of the 1997 animated film *Anastasia*, singing 'Journey to the Past', written by Lynn Ahrens and Stephen Flaherty. In 1998, the song was nominated for a Golden Globe Award as well as an Academy Award for Best Original Song, with Aaliyah performing her rendition live at the Oscars. That same year, she continued her film soundtrack contributions with the *Dr. Dolittle* track 'Are You That Somebody?' Featuring curious production, again from Timbaland, and coquettish lyrical assistance from Static Major, the song famously features a baby cooing in the background. Because of rules that were later adjusted on the Hot 100, the song was ineligible to chart for a significant portion of its shelf life but it still peaked at No. 1 on the R&B/ Hip-Hop Airplay chart and No. 21 on the Hot 100. Internationally, the song performed much more successfully, peaking at No. 1 in New Zealand, No. 3 in the Netherlands, and No. 11 on the UK Singles Chart.

In 1999, 'Are You That Somebody?' earned Aaliyah her first Grammy nomination for Best Female R&B Vocal Performance.

As she continued to work on her self-titled album, Aaliyah co-starred in her first film role, *Romeo Must Die*, released in 2000, alongside martial arts expert Jet Li. In addition to her starring role in the film, Aaliyah also served as co-executive producer of the soundtrack. She contributed to multiple songs, including the superhit 'Try Again', produced by Timbaland and written by Timbaland and Static Major. Over at times slick, at times warbling electronic-heavy sounds, Aaliyah encourages a potential suitor to remain persistent after initially being rejected. The song reached No. 1 on the Hot 100, Aaliyah's first; it also became the first single to top the chart based solely on airplay. The B-side of the single, 'Come Back in One Piece', features the high-octane Yonkers rapper DMX and

Aaliyah's 'Try Again' hit No. 1 on the Hot 100 in 2000, the singer's first and only chart-topper, and the first single to reach the peak based solely on airplay.

highlights Aaliyah's penchant for floating her soft-focus vocals over tough beats. "When I read an article, someone said 'Aaliyah's image and her style is street but sweet,'" Aaliyah told *Plus vite que la musique*. "I love that because it is a bit hard-edged, it is street, it's very raw – some of the tracks are very raw. So that someone like a DMX can get on the track and rap on it, and then I can come on the track and sing as well. And my voice is very sweet, it's a very simple, sweet, airy sort of sound. I think that's very fitting. It's street but sweet."

Working with Timbaland, Missy Elliott and Static Major at her side, in addition to other musicians and writers, Aaliyah took a more hands-on approach when crafting her ambitious self-titled project, which has also become known as 'The Red Album', due to its vibrant packaging. Her earlier works were successful, but not entirely self-inspired. With *Aaliyah*, the singer was able to tap into what she wanted for herself – and her scores of adoring fans. "I definitely wanted to take my time in making this album and to put my best foot forward and put 110 per cent into this for my fans," Aaliyah told *Plus vite que la musique*. "I aim to please them. I want to, of course, please myself and make good music, but I aim to please them. So I wasn't mad at the fact that I had the time to do that, and to go back over some of the songs that I had done before I even did *Romeo* and fix them and tweak them. So, I do feel that in the end it was great because I feel this is my best album. This is the best work that I've done so far."

An adventurous theatricality drove *Aaliyah*. The opening track and lead single, 'We Need A Resolution' with Timbaland, is cinema in audio form, Aaliyah going back and forth with her partner about trying to work through a failing, passive-aggressive relationship. The following single, 'Rock the Boat', saw Aaliyah singing about her desires in a more

Aaliyah effortlessly blended her sweet, airy vocals with futuristic, streetwise sounds, leading her to be christened the "Princess of R&B."

forthcoming way than fans were used to hearing. She had long been positioned as mature, but this album, and this song, represented Aaliyah's proper transition to womanhood. The music video was partially filmed in The Bahamas and sadly the plane departing the island carrying Aaliyah and eight others crashed on 25 August 2001, resulting in their untimely deaths. After consideration, Blackground chose to release the music video for 'Rock the Boat', as well as the following single 'More Than a Woman', the latter of which built on the futuristic foundation that Aaliyah had been assembling since *One In A Million*. Album tracks 'Never No More' and 'I Refuse' are two sides of the same tense, dramatic coin, the former telling a tale of domestic abuse and the latter homing in on the work of overcoming a broken heart.

Though there have been posthumous compilations, which included unreleased material like the bittersweet 'Miss You', 2001's *Aaliyah* remains the singer's last body of original work; it has since been certified double platinum. More assured than she had ever been, on it Aaliyah continually narrowed the vision she began with, further excavating her vocal abilities and shaping her own conceptual ideas. Aaliyah's impact continues to reverberate across the music industry, from direct descendants like Ciara and Ashanti to global titans like Drake and Beyoncé. "For those who have

Aaliyah

ALBUMS:
Age Ain't Nothing But a Number (1994)
One in a Million (1996)
Aaliyah (2001)

SONGS:
'Back & Forth' (1994)
'At Your Best (You Are Love)' (1994)
'If Your Girl Only Knew' (1996)
'One in a Million' (1996)
'4 Page Letter' (1997)
'Journey to the Past' (1997)
'The One I Gave My Heart To' (1997)
'Are You That Somebody' (1998)
'Try Again' (2000)
'We Need a Resolution' featuring
    Timbaland (2001)
'Rock the Boat' (2001)
'More Than a Woman' (2001)
'Never No More' (2001)
'I Refuse' (2001)
'Miss You' (2002)

met Aaliyah, I know she's touched y'all not just because of her passing, but just because of her spirit – the kind of spirit that she has," Missy Elliott said in the Grammy Awards press room in February 2002. "When she met people, she always left an imprint on them. It's most definitely a sad situation for our family, but I know for a fact that she's looking over us. I have dreams about her all the time; actually, it's crazy how many dreams that I have about her. I know that she's not here in body, but she's here in spirit."

"I'm the interpreter," Aaliyah told *USA Today* in July 2001. "I'm the one who takes your words and brings them to life. I was trained to sing and dance and laugh, and that's what I want to do."

Despite her short life, Aaliyah solidified her legacy as a visionary artist whose influence is still felt in contemporary music.

AALIYAH

AALIYAH, 'TRY AGAIN'

Release date: March 2000
Album: *Romeo Must Die* soundtrack
Recorded: 1999
Label: Blackground/Virgin
Studio: Manhattan Center (New York City)
Songwriters: Timothy 'Timbaland' Mosley, Stephen 'Static Major' Garrett
Billboard Hot 100: 1
UK Singles Chart: 8

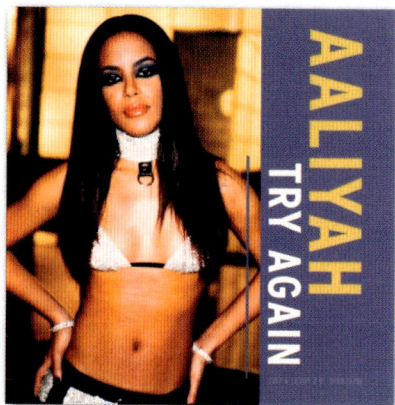

Critical Acclaim

In addition to her starring in her first film, *Romeo Must Die*, Aaliyah also served as co-executive producer of the soundtrack. She contributed to multiple songs, including the superhit 'Try Again.'

Recording

'Try Again' was produced by Timbaland and written by Timbaland and the late Static Major. In the song, Aaliyah encourages a potential suitor to remain persistent after initially being rejected – all performed over at times slick, at times warbling electronic-heavy sounds. The intro of the song, performed by Timbaland, contains an interpolation of Eric B. & Rakim's 'I Know You Got Soul.'

Legacy

'Try Again' was Aaliyah's first song to reach No. 1 on the Hot 100. It also became the first single to top the chart based solely on airplay. Aaliyah's nimble, expert navigation of Timbaland's futuristic production became the blueprint for other artists who followed in her footsteps, including direct descendants like Ciara and Ashanti and global titans like Drake and Beyoncé.

Remixes

Dutch DJ/producer D'Maduro remixed 'Try Again,' transforming the song into a future dancehall sonic adventure.

Covers

- **2017, Rag'n'Bone Man -** The UK singer reworked the single during a Spotify recording session with Spoon drummer Jim Eno, providing soulful vocals over Eno's minimal production.

BRANDY

From a young age, Brandy dreamed of being "as large as Whitney." "When I was 7, Whitney Houston caught my eye, and I was like, 'This lady is mad crazy! She's so, so beautiful'," Brandy told *Rome News-Tribune* in a July 1995 interview. "I just wanted to be like her. Not just the beauty, but her voice … she was very powerful, the way she'd sing a word like 'love' or 'mine'."

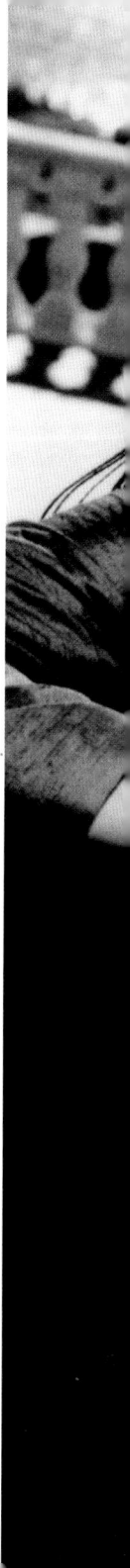

ittle did Brandy know, Whitney Houston would wind up becoming her eventual co-star and mentor. Taking on the role of Fairy Godmother to Brandy's Cinderella in the 1997 television film remake of the Rodgers and Hammerstein musical, Whitney Houston guided Brandy through projecting her voice more confidently and coming into her own as a performer. "Brandy was definitely hand-picked by me," Whitney Houston recalled to *Entertainment Tonight* in 1997. "I definitely wanted her to be Cinderella." "I've always wanted to sing with some of the people that I've looked up to, like Whitney," Brandy told *ET* in an interview from the same year. "Just to be in the studio with her, I just give it all I have, give it all I got." The two-hour Disney special drew in an estimated 60 million viewers, ABC's highest ratings in nearly two decades, the attentive audience feeling as enraptured by the princess experience as

> **I've always wanted to sing with some of the people that I've looked up to, like Whitney.**
> **BRANDY**

the woman expected to play the role. Initially, Houston was offered the role of Cinderella in 1993, but she passed after years went by, projects intervened and Houston had her own child. The programme wound up winning an Emmy for Outstanding Art Direction in a Variety, Musical or Comedy Special.

Learning first hand from one of music's most beloved powerhouse vocalists gave Brandy a leg up on her contemporaries – but she was never afraid to collaborate with her peers or even media-made adversaries. On her chart-topping 1998 duet 'The Boy Is Mine', Brandy exchanges words and impressive vocal riffs with then fellow-teen R&B singer Monica. The single became the first No. 1 hit for both artists, spending 13 consecutive weeks atop the Hot 100, going on to earn a Grammy for Best R&B Performance by a Duo or Group with Vocals in 1999.

It also was the bestselling single of 1998 in the US. Initially cowritten with LaShawn Daniels, Rodney 'Darkchild' Jerkins, Fred Jerkins III, Japhe Tejeda and Brandy, the song was produced by Darkchild with additional assistance from Dallas Austin. Its first iteration was a solo song featuring just Brandy's vocals – but the meticulous singer-songwriter knew that something felt off. "'The Boy Is Mine' was missing something," Brandy recounted onstage at Tyler Perry Studios during the 2020 Verzuz live music battle with Monica. "It just was; it was a great song, different. Rodney's amazing, LaShawn is amazing, but I felt like it was missing something and it was missing you [Monica]. I felt like what you brought to the song, it just took it to a different place. And that's why I hunted you down and asked you to be a part of this song. 'The Boy Is Mine' was actually my first single but I couldn't release it because I knew that it was missing you."

Known throughout the music industry as 'The Vocal Bible', a title that carries with it a great deal of weight and respect, Brandy aptly began her journey toward this acknowledgement when she sang her first solo in church aged two. Born in McComb, Mississippi in 1979, Brandy Rayana Norwood was raised in Carson, California by Willie Norwood, a choir director and gospel singer, and Sonja Norwood, a district manager for H&R Block who would go on to resign from her position in order to manage

Brandy is known throughout the music industry as 'The Vocal Bible', thanks to her dexterous singing abilities.

Brandy's fledgling career. "I knew Brandy was going to be a star the day she was born," Sonja glowingly told *People* magazine in a June 1998 issue. "I told the doctor that he had just delivered a star and that she was going to be something one day." As intuitive as Brandy's talent was to her parents, Brandy had difficulty as a freshman at the Hollywood High Performing Arts Center. Her classmates were being sent for auditions but Brandy's teacher wasn't affording her the same opportunities. "One day I asked, 'Why aren't you sending me out on calls?' and she said, 'Because you're not drop-dead gorgeous,'" Brandy told *People*. "My heart just dropped."

With a bruised ego and a resilient spirit, Brandy forged ahead, entering talent shows before she picked up a gig as a backing singer for the teen R&B group Immature. In 1993, her dream of being a superstar singer came true, but it conflicted with another dream that fell into her lap: her major label deal with Atlantic coincided with her first television role as Danesha, the daughter of the strong-willed, titular character of the sitcom *Thea*. "I had a difficult time on *Thea* because I never dreamed of being an actress," Brandy revealed to *Okayplayer* in July 2018. "I thought everyone was light years ahead of me. There was one moment where I felt right at home: It's when I was given the opportunity to sing and dance live on television as Thea's daughter." The show only lasted one season, a blessing in disguise for Brandy who sought to give her undivided attention to her music. "When *Thea* was canceled, I was like, 'Okay, I can now put all my focus into my album,'" Brandy told *Vibe* magazine in February 2011.

Brandy's self-titled debut album, largely produced by Keith Crouch, came out in September 1994. While it was a slow burner on the charts, it produced three top 10 hits. 'I Wanna Be Down', an innocent plea to

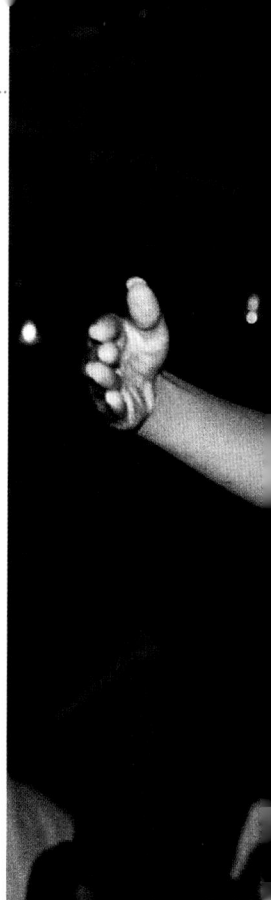

be allowed into her crush's life, peaked at No. 6 on the Hot 100 and No. 5 on the UK Hip Hop and R&B chart. "I knew I really made it when I was at this chicken spot in Carson with my friends," Brandy told *Vibe*. "One of the cars that pulled up was playing 'I Wanna Be Down'! That was it for me! My friends and I were so excited. You couldn't tell me nothing." Meanwhile, the follow-up single, 'Baby', a wolf whistle in song form, reached No. 4 in both the US and New Zealand. Both of these singles hit No. 1 on the Billboard Hot R&B/Hip-Hop Songs chart. 'Brokenhearted', a lovelorn ballad that was originally a solo effort, was

After overcoming early rejection, Brandy's journey to stardom culminated in her self-titled 1994 debut album, which positioned her as a rising force in R&B.

BRANDY

re-recorded as a duet with Wanya Morris from Boyz II Men and reached No. 9 on the Hot 100. The success of these songs lifted the sales of the album, which has now been certified quadruple platinum by the RIAA.

With her first hit records in tow, Brandy was tasked with crafting a new song for the *Waiting to Exhale* soundtrack, released in 1995. The film centred on a group of Black women experiencing the various stages of sisterhood and called for a song that represented the women finding their own versions of love. Brandy's contribution, the Babyface penned and

> **It was calling me – that's what normally happens when I'm ready to do music. It kind of tugs at me, it haunts me.**
>
> **BRANDY**

produced 'Sittin' Up in My Room', peaked at No. 2 on the Hot 100 and No. 3 on the UK Hip Hop and R&B chart, a testament to the smoky, alluring vocals that would come to be revered by her predecessors and successors alike.

In January 1996, Brandy's *Moesha* sitcom debuted. Based on the fictional life of a Black American teenager living with her upper middle class family, including a new stepmother, the TV show was set in Leimert Park, Los Angeles. The series, which extended until May 2001, focused on Moesha, a goody-two-shoes teen whose life couldn't be any more different from Brandy's. "I was too embarrassed to tell my mom about some of the things I was experiencing because of the good-girl image that had been created for me," Brandy told Oprah Winfrey in the July 2002 issue of *O* magazine. "I couldn't really express myself to anyone. The public thought, 'Brandy would never do this or that.' But I was doing those

'The Boy Is Mine,' Brandy's duet with fellow R&B singer Monica, became a chart-topping cultural phenomenon and a Grammy-winning hit.

things." When Winfrey asked what kinds of things Brandy was doing, she responded: "When I was 15, I fell in love with someone who was 20. When I tried to talk to [my] Mom about it, she said, 'You're not in love. You don't know what love is.'" With these contrasting expectations in front of her – one telling her that she was a grown adult and another telling her she was still too inexperienced – Brandy set out to discover the truth on her own.

Desiring a new direction that meshed well with her clean-girl image but gave her more agency, Brandy consulted with up-and-coming producer Rodney 'Darkchild' Jerkins on her five times platinum-selling follow-up album *Never Say Never*. Brandy picked up more songwriting and production credits here, including on her first No. 1 single 'The Boy Is Mine' featuring Monica, which flipped industry expectations on their head. Throughout *Never Say Never*, Brandy enforces a sound that is more ballad-heavy and adult contemporary, as opposed to the 'urban pop' sound that dominated her first project. While she did her best to eschew expectations, she still relied on the hip-hop partnership that bolstered her first album; 'Top of the World' with Bad Boy Records artist Mase gave Brandy a similar streetwise appeal to the one she garnered during her first project. The following singles, the Diane Warren-written, David Foster-produced 'Have You Ever' and the Rodney Jerkins-led 'Angel in Disguise', presented Brandy as an aware seeker of love, one who was as willing to put herself out there as much as she was willing to receive potential incoming receptions of reality; 'Have You Ever' became Brandy's first solo No. 1 hit.

In 1998, Brandy landed her first major theatrical film role in the slasher flick *I Still Know What You Did Last Summer*. The following year, she appeared in the TV movie *Double Platinum* with Diana Ross and continued her focus on *Moesha* until the show was cancelled in the spring of 2001. "Of course, I love acting, and I was really sad when *Moesha* ended – and how it ended, because I know a lot of the fans were

left basically with a cliffhanger," Brandy told *Billboard* in June 2022. "But I was really ready to get back to my music. I had been having conversations with the team, and I was working with Mike City, who did the title track for *Full Moon*. It was calling me – that's what normally happens when I'm ready to do music. It kind of tugs at me, it haunts me. So I was happy. It was sort of like an escape because of everything else that happened before. I wanted to go in with a clear mind and be ready to follow that creative spark that we all felt."

Full Moon was the indicative pinpoint of when Brandy transitioned from teen pop sensation into R&B front-runner and genre shaper. "*Full Moon* was an album that I knew I needed to step up my game," Brandy told *Billboard*. "I knew I needed to come out of my comfort zone and sing completely out of my range. I was squeezing and doing all kinds of stuff to hit the notes and really find the different emotions that made this

On her platinum-selling album *Never Say Never*, Brandy embraced a more mature sound and expanded her creative control.

album so different than my previous albums." The result of Brandy testing the limits of her abilities was an album that has stood the test of time for its elaborate harmony layering and vocal stacking. "For the second album, Rodney, LaShawn and the guys were open to me trying to do certain things with my voice," Brandy recalled to *Billboard*. "They already knew how I wanted to approach music on *Never Say Never*. But then on *Full Moon*, it was like freedom." Through songs like the ever-curious, decidedly amorous title track and the glitchy, forward-thinking lead single 'What About Us?' – itself peaking at No. 7 on the Hot 100 – Brandy demonstrated her capability of keeping up with the times and pushing the agenda forward.

With her 2003 project *Afrodisiac*, Brandy expanded further out, extending the branches of her creativity and providing additional paths for her offshoots to find their own way. The Kanye West-produced 'Talk About Our Love', which also featured the rapper, peaked at No. 6 on the UK

Brandy

ALBUMS:
Brandy (1994)
Never Say Never (1998)
Full Moon (2002)
Afrodisiac (2004)
Human (2008)
Two Eleven (2012)
B7 (2020)

SONGS:
'I Wanna Be Down' (1994)
'Baby' (1994)
'Brokenhearted' featuring Wanya Morris (1995)
'Sittin' Up in My Room' (1996)

'The Boy Is Mine' with Monica (1998)
'Top of the World' (1998)
'Have You Ever?' (1998)
'Angel in Disguise' (1999)
'Almost Doesn't Count' (1999)
'What About Us?' (2002)
'Full Moon' (2002)
'Talk About Our Love' featuring Kanye West (2004)
'Who Is She 2 U' (2004)
'Right Here (Departed)' (2008)
'Long Distance' (2008)
'Put It Down' featuring Chris Brown (2012)
'Love Again' with Daniel Caesar (2019)

Singles Chart, and the Timbaland-helmed, intentionally investigative 'Who Is She 2 U' reached No. 7 on the German Urban Charts. Her follow-up albums, 2008's *Human* and 2012's *Two Eleven*, represented a Brandy who was determined to remain inspired by contemporary sounds and lyrics ('Right Here (Departed)', 'Put It Down' featuring Chris Brown), while staying true to her soulful roots ('Long Distance'). On *B7*, released in 2020, Brandy fully confronts the moods and emotions expressed in previous albums, yet she takes them on with such a marked maturity ('Love Again' with Daniel Caesar) that it feels like a new experience in itself.

As The Vocal Bible, Brandy has inspired countless vocalists, including Ariana Grande, whom she collaborated with on 'The Boy Is Mine' remix alongside Monica. "I heard H.E.R. say to Tori Kelly once ... 'I felt like when I started listening to Brandy, I started singing better,'" Brandy told *Billboard*. "And this is H.E.R., she's amazing! And Tori Kelly, Ariana Grande – these are real vocalists. For them to pay homage in their way and to be influenced and still find their own style and make it their own, it's just unbelievable. Wow, I'm flattered. It could bring me to tears, especially when it's artists that are like that and they really appreciate it."

With *Full Moon*, Brandy evolved from teen pop star to skilled R&B reformer, pushing her vocal and sonic boundaries to innovate a genre-defining sound that would influence a generation of artists.

BRANDY

BRANDY AND MONICA, 'THE BOY IS MINE'

Release date: May 4, 1998
Album: *Never Say Never*
Recorded: 1997
Label: Atlantic
Studio: Record One (Los Angeles);
DARP (Atlanta)
Songwriters: LaShawn Daniels, Rodney
'Darkchild' Jerkins, Fred Jerkins III,
Japhe Tejeda and Brandy Norwood
Billboard Hot 100: 1
UK Singles Chart: 2

Critical Acclaim

Brandy was never afraid to collaborate with her peers – or even media-made adversaries. On her chart-topping 1998 duet 'The Boy Is Mine', she exchanges words and impressive vocal riffs with then-fellow teen R&B singer Monica.

Recording

Initially co-written by LaShawn Daniels, Rodney 'Darkchild' Jerkins, Fred Jerkins III, Japhe Tejeda and Brandy, the song was produced by Darkchild with additional assistance from Dallas Austin. Originally it was recorded as a solo song featuring just Brandy's vocals, but she knew that something felt off. During the 2020 Verzuz live music battle with Monica, Brandy said that "I felt like it was missing something and it was missing you [Monica]. I felt like what you brought to the song, it just took it to a different place. And that's why I hunted you down and asked you to be a part of this song. 'The Boy Is Mine' was actually my first single but I couldn't release it because I knew that it was missing you."

Legacy

The single became the first No. 1 hit for both Brandy and Monica, and spent 13 consecutive weeks atop the *Billboard* Hot 100. 'The Boy Is Mine' was the bestselling single of 1998 in the US, and went on to earn a Grammy for Best R&B Performance by a Duo or Group with Vocals in 1999.

Remixes

UK garage group Architechs had a career breakthrough after producing a skittering, modular remix of 'The Boy Is Mine.' British production duo 99 Souls crafted 'The Girl Is Mine,' a house mash-up of the single and Destiny's Child's 'Girl' that, after being officially approved and re-released with new vocals from Brandy, reached No. 5 on the UK Singles chart.

Covers

- **2010, *Glee* cast -** Amber Riley and Naya Rivera performed the song in the episode 'Laryngitis.'
- **2018, Postmodern Jukebox -** The rotating musical collective released a vintage 1940s version which has been viewed more than 2 million times on YouTube.
- **2024, Ariana Grande -** The megastar pop singer reimagined the song as a solo track, and later released a remix with Brandy and Monica.

DESTINY'S
CHILD

Destiny's Child left no room for confusion when it came to their group name. Motivated by sheer will and a searing hope of self-fulfilling prophecy, the fluctuating Houston-based band was determined to make a name for itself.

M oulded early on by Mathew Knowles, an equipment sales executive, and his wife Tina, a successful hair salon owner, Destiny's Child was originally known as Girls Tyme. The Knowles' eldest daughter Beyoncé was winning singing and performance competitions across the state of Texas, and they were looking to elevate her talent and take her exposure to the next level. In 1990, Beyoncé and LaTavia Roberson, both nine years old, met at an audition and became fast friends. After meeting, the two young artists became members of the multimember group Girls Tyme, who worked with producers Arne Frager and Alonzo Jackson. *Destiny's Child: The Untold Story Presents Girls Tyme* was released in 2019 by Mathew Knowles and features writing and production credits by Frager and Jackson. The contents of the album, particularly the lyrics, sound intentionally childish, but the delivery of the overall music is ambitious, if not precocious.

The group would perform for anyone who would listen to them, including patrons at Tina's hair salon. Over time, Girls Tyme generated

Destiny's Child was formed and developed by Beyoncé's parents, and originally went by the name Girls Tyme.

enough attention to appear on the nationally televised programme *Star Search* in the autumn of 1992; by this time, Kelendria 'Kelly' Rowland had joined the lineup. Presented as a six-member group, including dancers, the band performed 'Talking 'Bout My Baby', a New Jack Swing-influenced song that saw the girls singing and rapping about puppy love. Girls Tyme ended up losing to a male rock band that was three times their age, receiving a tally of three out of four compared to the rock band's perfect score. In the opinion of the Girls Tyme members and their early backers, the song choice was simply off; "This was a hip-hop thing and *Star Search* didn't even know what hip-hop was," Tina said in VH1's 2003 documentary *Driven: Beyoncé*.

> **We got the word 'destiny' out of the Bible, but we couldn't trademark the name, so we added 'child,' which is like a rebirth of destiny.**
>
> **BEYONCÉ**

Determined to push the girls forward, Mathew took management control of the group and put the artists through an unofficial summer boot camp; at this point, LeToya Luckett had joined Beyoncé, LaTavia and Kelly, and they became a solidified quartet. "It was just continual artist development," Mathew said. "I would jog with them in the morning, and they would sing while they were jogging to build up their stamina. There were vocal lessons; a choreographer would come in in the afternoons. Tina and I eventually built a deck patio in our backyard that became their stage." In addition to Mathew's hands-on managing, Tina did the girls' hair and designed their performance attire. The group's name morphed through different iterations, before its members settled on Destiny's Child in 1996. "We got the word 'destiny' out of the Bible, but we couldn't trademark the name, so we added 'child,' which is like a rebirth of destiny," Beyoncé Knowles-Carter told *CBS News* in 2002.

After getting signed to, then dropped from, Elektra Records, Destiny's Child again faced an unexpected industry set-back – but Mathew quit his corporate job and invested even more time, money and energy into making Destiny's Child into stars. Now properly serving as the group's manager, Knowles called on Teresa LaBarbera Whites, former talent scout for Columbia Records, who had flown to Houston to see Destiny's Child perform as younger artists and ultimately was unsuccessful in signing them. LaBarbera Whites was determined to sign Destiny's Child this time around and had them perform a showcase for all of the department heads at the label. "Once Columbia actually got a chance to see them perform, in a room with all the big cats ... they blew them away," contributing songwriter and producer D'Wayne Wiggins said in the VH1 documentary. Destiny's Child was signed but that wasn't the end of their worries: they then had to produce the hits they had long been so sure they were capable of making.

After being signed and dropped, Destiny's Child secured another deal and released their self-titled, platinum-certified debut album in 1998.

Destiny's Child, the group's debut 1998 album, was preceded by the lead single 'No, No, No'. A slow jam about the art of seduction, the single was remixed by the former Fugees member Wyclef Jean, who injected the song with brash, in-your-face production that forced the girls to adapt their delivery. The remix was a success, reaching No. 3 on the Hot 100 and No. 1 on the Billboard Hot R&B/Hip-Hop Songs chart. This new clipped style of singing, made for an uptempo change of pace, would influence Destiny's Child's approach as a whole, rippling out toward other artists and subgenres, but on their self-titled debut, they mainly stuck to an overly sophisticated neo-soul sound. "The first record was successful but not hugely successful," Beyoncé told *The Guardian* in 2006. "It was a neo-soul record and we were 15 years old. It was way too mature for us." Erring toward unearned maturity or not, the album was bolstered by the success of 'No, No, No', eventually earning an RIAA platinum certification for both the song and the album.

Excited to have made an impression but still unsatiated, Beyoncé, Kelly, LaTavia and LeToya went back into the studio, this time with the hot producers of the moment, Kevin 'She'kspere' Briggs and Rodney 'Darkchild' Jerkins, and the fiery Kandi Burruss as a songwriter. In July 1999, Destiny's Child released *The Writing's on the Wall*, which became the group's breakthrough album. Introduced as leaders of their respective faux mob families, the women used the album to run down Destiny's Child's commandments of relationships. "Thou shalt not hate," Beyoncé says immediately before 'So Good', a precursor to the blippy, catchy, almost digital sound that would come to dominate the 2000s. 'Bills, Bills, Bills', a quirky, sassy, go-to song for any woman

> " We had no idea that *The Writing's on the Wall* would be as big a record as it was.
>
> **BEYONCÉ**

dealing with a broke and/or stingy partner, was the lead single of *The Writing's on the Wall* and became Destiny's Child's first No. 1 single on the Hot 100. Produced by Briggs and written by Burruss, Beyoncé, LeToya and Kelly, 'Bills, Bills, Bills' featured the playful singing style that would come to dominate hip-hop and R&B, as well as pop. "That staccato, fast singing has kind of become the sound of R&B," Beyoncé told *The Guardian*. "It's still here in 2006, but we had no idea of what its impact would be. We had no idea that *The Writing's on the Wall* would be as big a record as it was."

In December 1999, LeToya Luckett and LaTavia Roberson attempted to break away from Mathew Knowles as their manager, citing their belief that he was keeping an unfair amount of the group's profits and that he openly favoured his daughter Beyoncé and Kelly Rowland. While LeToya and LaTavia were only seeking to explore their options with outside management, their request was seen as a personal

attack, and they were replaced by new members Michelle Williams and Farrah Franklin. Finding out about their replacements when the music video for 'Say My Name' debuted in February 2000, Luckett and Roberson sued Mathew Knowles – and Beyoncé and Kelly – for

Destiny's Child's breakthrough album, 1999's *The Writing's on the Wall*, cemented the group's signature R&B sound amid internal conflicts and lineup changes.

breach of partnership and fiduciary duties. The case against the girls was eventually dropped and a settlement was reached with Mathew, but there was no coming back for LeToya and LaTavia. Five months after joining Destiny's Child, Farrah Franklin left the group, with Beyoncé stating in the press that she had missed multiple promotional dates and couldn't handle the pressure, and Franklin herself stating the vibes in the group were 'negative' and she had limited creative control. "It is definitely tough," Beyoncé told *Time* magazine in January 2001. "A lot of people don't have any concept of how many sacrifices we have to make. You have to accept it, because if you don't, you won't last."

While 'Say My Name' was swimming in controversy, the song became the best-performing single from *The Writing's on the Wall*, hitting No. 1 on the Billboard Hot 100 and No. 3 on the UK Singles Chart, as well as earning a triple platinum certification. Additionally, Destiny's Child won two Grammy Awards for 'Say My Name': Best R&B Vocal Performance by a Duo or Group and Best R&B Song. The album, meanwhile, went octuple platinum in the US; it remains Destiny's Child's highest-selling album. Moving forward with the three women lineup of Beyoncé, Kelly and Michelle, Destiny's Child was selected to produce a theme song for the 2000 film *Charlie's Angels*. 'Independent Women Part 1', a rugged, yet soaring anthem that called for ample amounts of female empowerment, was released as a single in October of 2000. After ascending the chart, the song spent 11 consecutive weeks at No. 1 on the Hot 100, the longest-running single that year and of Destiny's Child's career to date. The single also reached No. 1 on the UK Singles Chart.

With an expectation to deliver on the follow-up to the massively huge *The Writing's on the Wall*, the group chose to lean into the widespread

'Say My Name' became one of Destiny's Child's best-performing singles, hitting No. 1 on the Billboard Hot 100, and earning triple platinum status and two Grammy Awards.

publicity surrounding the personnel switch-up, which was exacerbated by barbs exchanged between both sides in the media. As the remaining members of Destiny's Child recall, a radio DJ was cracking jokes about members of the group voting each other off of an island, similar to the reality show *Survivor*. "There was this DJ that made up a joke about us, you know: Who's going to be the last Destiny's Child member on the island?" Kelly Rowland recounted in the VH1 documentary. "[Beyoncé] was like, 'Oh, you wanna make jokes? [Sings] *I'm a survivor*.'" The resulting album, aptly titled *Survivor*, was led by the string-driven, cinematic title track, which hit No. 1 on the UK Singles Chart and No. 2 on the Hot 100. 'Bootylicious', the Stevie Nicks-sampling, funked-out, jargon-building jam, reached No. 2 on the UK Singles

> **A lot of people don't have any concept of how many sacrifices we have to make. You have to accept it, because if you don't, you won't last.**
>
> **BEYONCÉ**

Chart and No. 1 on the Billboard Hot 100 – as of 2025, it remains the last single by a girl group to top the Hot 100. Boosted by the successful singles and Destiny's Child's penchant for crafting music for both hype and emotional environments, *Survivor* sold 663,000 units in its first week, placing Destiny's Child atop the Billboard 200 for the first time; the album has since been certified quadruple platinum.

Toward the end of 2001, the members of Destiny's Child announced that they would be working on a series of side projects planned to be released in a staggered schedule. The first solo project was Michelle's debut *Heart to Yours*, a gospel album released in April 2002 that included a duet with gospel titan Shirley Caesar. That October, Kelly released her own debut, *Simply Deep*, an assertive, alternative R&B project, but it was

'Dilemma', the signature situationship song with Nelly, that won Kelly a 2003 Grammy Award for Best Rap/Sung Collaboration. Beyoncé released her own highly anticipated debut, *Dangerously in Love*, in June of 2003, and it built further on the songwriting and producing skills Beyoncé had been acquiring throughout her career with Destiny's Child. The album, an evenly weighted endeavour that combined soul, R&B and hip-hop elements, debuted atop the Billboard 200, selling 317,000 copies in its first week, and going on to earn a seven times platinum certification. Beyoncé also won five Grammy Awards at the 2004 ceremony: Best Contemporary R&B Album; Best R&B Performance by a Duo or Group with Vocals ('The Closer I Get to You' with Luther Vandross); Best Female R&B Vocal Performance ('Dangerously in Love 2'); and Best R&B Song and Best Rap/Sung Collaboration ('Crazy in Love' with Jay-Z).

Destiny's Child embraced the attention of their personnel switch-up with their successful *Survivor* album, which topped the Billboard 200 chart and went quadruple platinum.

Despite their individual successes, the trio reunited for *Destiny Fulfilled*, released in late 2004. "We did this record for ourselves, not to sell a million the first week out," Beyoncé told *Billboard* in 2004. "That doesn't mean as much to us as just the fact that three friends got back together to do another record. That was our destiny." The lead single, 'Lose My Breath', sounded like a marching band come to life, and featured each member singing their own written material in equal measure. The song peaked at No. 3 on the Hot 100 and No. 2 on the UK Singles Chart, its infectious live sound sticking to the ribs of listeners. *Destiny Fulfilled* was more solidly R&B than any Destiny's Child project, as previous albums ventured into rambunctious hip-hop and exploratory pop territories. The members' voices intertwine in luscious harmonies on songs like 'T-Shirt', 'If', and 'Girl', before separating into their own silos of vocal leadership ('Is She The Reason', 'Cater 2 U', 'Soldier'). Working alongside some of the industry's most sought-after songwriters and producers (9th Wonder, Bryan-Michael Cox, Sean Garrett) as well as musicians they had already experienced success with (Rodney Jerkins), Destiny's Child achieved a sound that was as progressive as it was grounded.

Destiny's Child

ALBUMS:
Destiny's Child (1998)
The Writing's on the Wall (1999)
Survivor (2001)
Destiny Fulfilled (2004)

SONGS:
'No, No, No' (1997)
'Bills, Bills, Bills' (1999)
'Bug a Boo' (1999)
'Say My Name' (2000)
'Jumpin' Jumpin'' (2000)
'Independent Women Part 1' (2000)
'Survivor' (2001)
'Bootylicious' (2001)
'Lose My Breath' (2004)
'Soldier' featuring T.I. and Lil Wayne (2004)
'T-Shirt' (2004)
'If' (2004)
'Is She The Reason' (2004)
'Girl' (2005)
'Cater 2 U' (2005)

In June 2005, Destiny's Child announced that they would be disbanding for good, but the group has come back together for specific purposes and performances. During Beyoncé's Super Bowl XLVII halftime show in 2013, and again five years later during her headlining Coachella set (affectionately called Beychella), Destiny's Child reunited as a trio. At Beyoncé's *Renaissance* tour stop in Houston in 2023, all of the group's members (excluding Farrah Franklin) were in attendance, a display of unity after years of interpersonal struggles. "That's what's beautiful," LeToya Luckett told *The Terrell Show* in 2023. "When people can just continue through life doing their thing, remove the negativity, not living in the past. Heal – time heals all wounds. It must have been, God planned it that way. I'm not going to question the Lord."

After its members achieved solo success, Destiny's Child reunited for 2004's *Destiny Fulfilled*, emphasizing friendship over sales before officially disbanding in 2005.

DESTINY'S CHILD, 'SAY MY NAME'

Release date: October 14, 1999
Album: *The Writing's on the Wall*
Recorded: 1999
Label: Columbia
Studio: Pacifique (North Hollywood)
Songwriters: Beyoncé Knowles, LeToya Luckett, LaTavia Roberson, Kelly Rowland, LaShawn Daniels, Fred Jerkins III, and Rodney 'Darkchild' Jerkins
Billboard Hot 100: 1
UK Singles Chart: 3

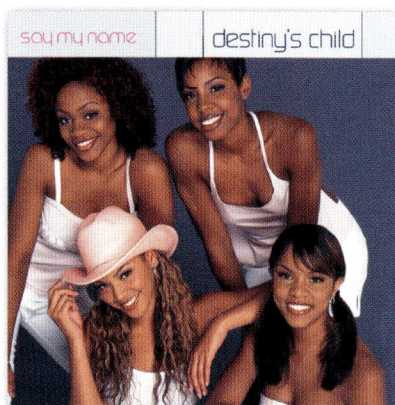

Critical Acclaim

Similar to Destiny's Child's first *Billboard* Hot 100 chart-topper, 'Bills, Bills, Bills,' 'Say My Name' featured a playful singing style that would come to dominate hip-hop and R&B. 'That staccato, fast singing has kind of become the sound of R&B,' Beyoncé told *The Guardian* in 2006.

Recording

'Say My Name' was Destiny's Child's first collaboration with R&B superproducer and songwriter Darkchild. Initially inspired by UK garage, the track was busy and brimmed with conflicting elements that turned the girls off, most notably Beyoncé. The group wrote to the track, but it was clear to everyone that this song wasn't going to make the album. Undaunted, Darkchild re-worked the production in the eleventh hour, and when Destiny's Child heard the new version, they loved it immediately.

Legacy

'Say My Name' became the best-performing single from *The Writing's on the Wall*, hitting No. 1 on the *Billboard* Hot 100 and No. 3 on the UK Singles Chart, as well as earning a triple platinum certification. Additionally, Destiny's Child won two Grammy Awards for the song: Best R&B Vocal Performance by a Duo or Group and Best R&B Song.

Remixes

The official mixes and remixes of 'Say My Name' include a Timbaland Remix featuring Static Major, Maurice's Last Days of Disco Millenium Mix and Daddy D Remix. There is also an alternate version of the song featuring a verse from the late basketball player Kobe Bryant.

Covers

- **2007, Superchunk -** The North Carolina indie rock band turned the R&B/pop song into a punk anthem.
- **2013, Drake -** Alongside singer-songwriter James Fauntleroy, the Toronto artist interpolates the song's catchy chorus and transforms it into the foundation for a lovelorn song.
- **2016, Alex & Sierra -** The Los Angeles pop duo initially covered the song on *The X Factor (US)*, later releasing their version in an EP titled *As Seen on TV*. It has amassed more than 15 million views on YouTube.
- **2019, Hozier -** The Irish singer-songwriter released an unhurried, soulful cover as a Spotify Single.

ASHANTI

Timing is everything. Ashanti, the First Lady of Murder Inc., knew that better than anyone when she became the first artist since The Beatles to have her first three entries chart in the top 10 of the Billboard Hot 100 simultaneously. But even with ample success scattered around her, Ashanti felt there had to be more to it.

“The initial success of 'Foolish', 'Always On Time' and 'What's Luv?' was just really weird for me because I didn't know," Ashanti told *Grammy.com* in October 2019. "I would always ask like, 'Is this good, guys? Are we doing good?' I really didn't understand it. And it's weird because I'm a humble person, and even back then I was a little naïve, you know. We were making history and we were on the top of the charts and everyone around me, all the guys are like, 'Yeah!' and I'm like, 'Oh, so this is a good thing.'" While she may not have been aware at the moment, Ashanti would come to understand the magnitude of her tenure with Murder Inc. as her career progressed – but she's still in constant pursuit of something greater. "I'm very proud and content with what I've accomplished in my career," she said on the *Angie Martinez IRL* podcast in October 2022. "But I'm always trying to do more and do better. And sometimes, people take

Ashanti was directly inspired by Mary J. Blige's invention of the hip-hop soul subgenre, a deliberate marriage of rap and R&B.

it as I'm unappreciative. They're like, 'Yo, you gotta slow down and appreciate the moment.' And I'm like, 'I did. And now I want to get a *new* moment.'"

Born in 1980 in Glen Cove, New York, Ashanti Shequoiya Douglas was raised by Tina, a former dance teacher, and Ken-Kaide, a former singer. Ashanti got her first taste of the spotlight as a young girl. "I wouldn't exactly say it's a gospel background, but of course I grew up in the church," Ashanti told NBC's *The Source: All Access* in 2002. "We had a little group called the Sun Beams, First Baptist Church. My mother made me go every Sunday, I was like five or six." While her innate talents were apparent from an early age, it wasn't until she turned 12 that she knew she wanted to be a singer. It was all an accident, per *Ashanti: The Making Of A Star*, released in February 2007. "I was doing chores downstairs in

> " I'm very proud and content with what I've accomplished in my career. But I'm always trying to do more and do better.
>
> **ASHANTI**

the living room," Ashanti explained. "My mom was like, 'Don't listen to the radio, no television.' She comes stomping down the steps, flying. She's like, 'What was that? I told you no radio.' I'm like, 'That was no radio, that was me singing.' And she's like, 'What? Let me hear it again.' So I sang and it was Mary J. Blige's 'Reminisce'." Prior to Blige, Ashanti couldn't identify a clear inspiration whose career she could model her own after. Once Ashanti was introduced to Blige's music, her dreams changed. "To be honest, I would have to say the person that really, really, really, really made me say, 'You know what? I think I want to do this,' would have to be Mary – Mary J. Blige," Ashanti told *The Source: All Access*. "I was like, there's nothing really out there that's in the middle. I didn't want to do ballad songs, and I didn't want to rhyme, and for me, she's the

ASHANTI

person that brought that marriage together. She had a hot, urban beat and she was singing, so I was like, 'Oh! It can work.'"

Shortly after discovering her gift, Ashanti began singing in talent shows and small festivals and her mother began sending out demo tapes. In 1992, she appeared as a child extra in Spike Lee's *Malcolm X*; the following year, she popped up in Ted Demme's hip-hop buddy comedy/thriller *Who's the*

After participating in talent shows and picking up small roles in movies and music videos, Ashanti was courted and rejected by multiple record labels before persevering under producer Irv Gotti's guidance.

Man? which starred Doctor Dré and Ed Lover of *Yo! MTV Raps* fame. She also had small parts in music videos, including KRS-One's 1995 single 'MC's Act Like They Don't Know' and 8-Off's 'Ghetto Girl', also released in 1995. Around this time, Ashanti was being courted by multiple record labels. "I done been through three record deals already, I started when I was 14," Ashanti said during a *Soul Train* interview in 2002. "It was a lot of doors slammed and all that, but you just have to stay persistent and surround yourself around people who genuinely care about you. Because there are so many snakes out there."

Ashanti's first opportunity to prove herself on wax came under the wing of producer and Murder Inc. label head Irv Gotti. "What I did tell her was, be a studio rat," Gotti says of Ashanti's early days. "I have this studio: just come to this studio. I was like, 'If you want to work, just come to the studio. Just come to the studio.' And she listened to that. The way she carried herself amongst the den of wolves – in the studio at any given time, 50 to 100 dudes. Gangstas, thugs, no one ever disrespected her. Everyone loved her like she was their little sister." Gotti coproduced Big Pun's posthumous 2001 single 'How We Roll' with Tru Stylze. As a featured artist, Ashanti's voice twinkles alongside Pun's nimble wordplay, boosting the emotional strength of the track. From this moment forward, Ashanti began writing hooks and performing duets with Gotti's web of interconnected MCs, effectively becoming the R&B darling to hip-hop's edgiest hustlers. "I think with Ashanti, she has a different appeal than just any R&B artist," Kim Osorio, former Editor-in-Chief of *The Source* magazine said in *Ashanti: The Making Of A Star*. "She had this appeal: not just to R&B fans and R&B music, but more so to hip-hop. That's what I think really made it set in because it reminded me of Mary J. Blige. When she came out, back in the early '90s, the way she was received by the hip-hop audience was like, 'That's not just R&B music.' It was hip-hop, she was just singing, and that's what I felt with Ashanti, also."

ASHANTI

Ashanti was featured on the 2001 *The Fast and the Furious* soundtrack, which was helmed by Irv Gotti. In the solo effort 'When a Man Does Wrong', carried by contemplative production, she homed in on the insecurities that come with a failed relationship. Elsewhere on the soundtrack, she appeared as a background vocalist for Caddillac Tah's 'Pov City Anthem' and as a featured artist on Vita's rap-centred remake of Madonna's 1990 single 'Justify My Love'. In November of 2001, Ja Rule released 'Always on Time', produced by 7 Aurelius and featuring Ashanti. "We were looking to put Brandy on 'Always on Time', or Beyoncé or Alicia Keys," Ja Rule revealed in a March 2024 episode of TV One's *Uncensored*. "[Ashanti] was sitting in the studio, writing her ass off, just waiting to get a real opportunity. Before that, she had done the [Big] Pun record, but there was no visual for her to the record. She wasn't in the video. So I was like, 'Okay, why are we not using her for this record and she's in-house?

In early 2002, Ashanti became a major force in R&B and hip-hop when she simultaneously held three spots in the top 10 of the Billboard Hot 100, a feat previously achieved only by The Beatles.

She's our artist.' We were thinking everything *big* for me. In my heart, I'm like, 'I'm already big. I could help break another artist with my bigness.'" Ashanti's delicate, yet assertive delivery on 'Always on Time' introduced the singer to a voracious world that was looking for a new sound from a new artist. The single topped the Hot 100 for two weeks in February and March 2002, confirming Murder Inc.'s impending dominance as a label.

February 2002 also brought a new single from Big Pun's close confidante Fat Joe, who released 'What's Luv?' produced by Irv Gotti and Murder Inc. mainstay Chink Santana. Ashanti featured on the track, which was characterized by a Y2K-inspired beat and a flirtatious theme. The banter and energetic interplay between the two artists boosted the song to No. 2 on the Hot 100 and No. 4 on the UK Singles Chart. That same month, Ashanti released her debut single, 'Foolish'. Built on an ambitious,

> **[Ashanti] was sitting in the studio, writing her ass off, just waiting to get a real opportunity.**
> **JA RULE**

generous sampling of DeBarge's 1983 song 'Stay With Me' – the same sample that The Notorious B.I.G. used for his own successful 1995 single 'One More Chance' – 'Foolish' became Ashanti's first solo No. 1, sitting atop the US chart for 10 weeks; this track officially brought Ashanti into the Murder Inc. fold as a signee. With 'Foolish' at No. 1 and 'Always on Time' and 'What's Luv?' occupying other spaces in the top 10, this is when Ashanti executed the music industry hat trick that only The Beatles had accomplished before. In March 2002, J. Lo's 'Ain't It Funny (Murder Remix)', on which Ashanti had significantly contributed as a songwriter, reached No. 1 on the Hot 100, giving Ashanti another significant win on the charts.

With multiple runaway hits on her hands, Ashanti released her cowritten, self-titled album in April 2002. It debuted at No. 1 on the Billboard 200,

selling 503,000 copies in its first week. This feat set a then record for the biggest opening week of sales for a woman artist's debut album in the US. Other singles, including 'Happy', which landed at No. 8 on the Hot 100 and No. 13 on the UK Singles Chart, and 'Baby', at No. 15 on the US chart, and deep cuts like 'Leaving (Always On Time Part II)' and 'Movies', rounded out an album that focused on unhealthy attachments, bliss and everything in between. On 'Happy', Ja Rule describes Ashanti as the "new princess of hip-hop and R&B," a declaration that ruffled the feathers of fans of the late Aaliyah, but ultimately stuck thanks to Ashanti being in high demand. "Yeah, we get calls about me being on people's records," Ashanti told *Hip Online* in November 2002. "We have to tone that down for a while. It's weird. Just to see how everything happened so quickly and to know everything was on the other side just a minute ago." *Ashanti* went on to be certified triple platinum and received the Grammy Award in 2003 for Best Contemporary R&B Album.

Ashanti's self-titled album sold over half a million copies in its first week, setting a then-record for biggest opening week of sales for a woman artist's debut album in the US.

The whirlwind of the industry experience didn't deter Ashanti – if anything, it galvanized her. She released her follow-up, *Chapter II*, in July 2003, with a continued focus on Irv Gotti and Chink Santana's in-house productions. It topped the Billboard 200, selling more than 326,000 copies in the first week. The album's lead single, 'Rock Wit U (Awww Baby)', was a bass-heavy island vibe that featured Ashanti singing about her expectations and desires and reached No. 2 in the US, No. 4 in Canada and No. 7 in the UK. The follow-up single, 'Rain on Me', reached No. 7 on the Hot 100, underscored by the message of overcoming domestic violence. *Chapter II*, with its deep relatability and intentional musicality, earned a platinum certification from the RIAA.

In September 2004, Ashanti was a guest vocalist on Ja Rule's 'Wonderful', also featuring R. Kelly; the song peaked at No. 1 on the UK Singles Chart and No. 5 on the Hot 100. That December, Ashanti released *Concrete Rose*, inspired by 2Pac's pseudonym 'The Rose That Grew From Concrete'. It debuted at No. 7 on the Billboard 200, despite selling 254,000 copies in its first week. The lead single was 'Only U', a rock-infused track produced by 7 Aurelius and Irv Gotti that samples Club Nouveau's 1986 song 'Why You Treat Me So Bad'. "It was really a different record for me," Ashanti told *BlackFilm.com* in December 2004. "With me being a person that likes to take a challenge, it was really important because it's my third album and we had a lot of success with the first album and with the second album I wanted to do something really different because that's what keeps people interested in you; when you are making different kinds of moves and you're succeeding with it. It was a little scary and we didn't know what was going to happen but it all worked out and I'm really excited about it." 'Only U' reached No. 13 on the Hot 100 and No. 2 on the UK Singles Chart, eventually earning a gold certification. Shortly after, Ashanti experimented with her acting career, making her film debut in 2005's *Coach Carter* and starring as Dorothy in the made-for-TV movie *The Muppets' Wizard of Oz*. The following year, she co-starred in the teen comedy *John Tucker Must Die* and, in 2007, she appeared in *Resident Evil: Extinction*.

After experiencing difficulties with Murder Inc. during and following 2008's *The Declaration*, Ashanti was released from the label by Irv Gotti. "The relationship has run its course," Gotti explained to MTV in May 2009. "The chemistry of what's needed – we're in two totally different places. You're talking to somebody that took her and shaped and moulded her and put her out there for the world, and it blew up. ... My views and philosophies and her views and philosophies are not meeting up." Subsequently, Ashanti decided to go the independent route, releasing her own music through her new label Written Entertainment. "I had offers from seven majors

Ashanti

ALBUMS:
Ashanti (2002)
Chapter II (2003)
Concrete Rose (2004)
The Declaration (2008)
Braveheart (2014)

SONGS:
'When a Man Does Wrong' (2001)
'Vita, Justify My Love' (2001)
'Ja Rule, Always on Time' (2001)
'Fat Joe, What's Luv?' (2002)
'Foolish' (2002)
'Leaving (Always On Time Part II)' (2002)
'Movies' (2002)
'Happy' (2002)
'Baby' (2002)
'Rock wit U (Awww Baby)' (2003)
'Rain on Me' (2003)
'Ja Rule, Wonderful' (2004)
'Only U' (2004)
'Good Good' (2008)
'Body on Me' featuring Nelly and Akon (2008)
'Never Should Have' (2014)
'I Got It' featuring Rick Ross (2014)

at one time and it was really hard to sit, you know, me being Libra, and be like, 'Okay, what should I do? Where should I go? I don't know what to do,'" Ashanti told *Grammy.com*. "And at that time, the labels were offering 360 deals, and I'm just not a fan of that, that's not my thing. So I made the very bold decision and scary decision to go independent … So I think just learning to trust myself, learning to be motivated to say, 'Hey, your future is in your hands and your destiny,' is really important. You have to kind of be in the driver's seat and know what's going on. It's very hard being the executive and the artist."

Ashanti's follow-up album, 2014's *Braveheart*, featured heartrending tracks like 'Never Should Have' and more upbeat songs like the Rick Ross-assisted 'I Got It'. The project reached No. 10 on the Billboard 200 and remains Ashanti's most recent album. Irv Gotti passed away in February 2025, leaving his relationship with Ashanti unresolved. "I really wanted to [be able to make peace with him before he passed] because like I said, we made history together," Ashanti told *Vibe* magazine in March 2025. "That is infinite. Like, talking about my son – my son is gonna know that we made these records together! I'm sad that the last few years we weren't seeing eye-to-eye. What I do know is that I tried. I do know that I extended the olive branch."

Ashanti's edgy, guitar-riff heavy 2004 single 'Only U' reached No. 2 on the UK Singles Chart.

ASHANTI, 'FOOLISH'

Release date: February 11, 2002

Album: *Ashanti*

Recorded: 2002

Label: Murder Inc./Def Jam

Studio: Crack House (New York City)

Songwriters: Ashanti, Mark DeBarge, Etterlene Jordan, Irving 'Irv Gotti' Lorenzo, Marcus '7 Aurelius' Vest

Billboard Hot 100: 1

UK Singles Chart: 4

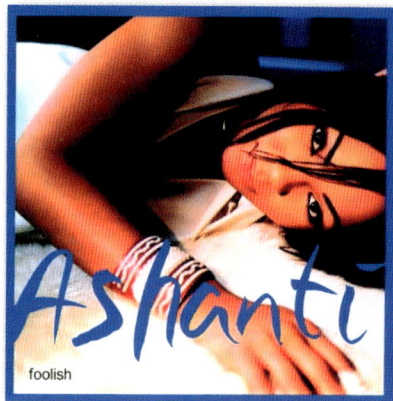

Critical Acclaim

'Foolish' became Ashanti's first solo No. 1, sitting atop the US chart for 10 weeks – at the same time that two of her other singles, the Ja Rule collaboration 'Always on Time' and the Fat Joe duet 'What's Luv?' occupied other spaces in the top 10. With this moment of overlap, Ashanti executed a music industry hat trick previously achieved only by The Beatles.

Recording

Produced by Irv Gotti and 7 Aurelius, 'Foolish' is built on an ambitious, generous sampling of DeBarge's 1983 song 'Stay With Me' – the same sample that The Notorious B.I.G. used for his own successful 1995 single 'One More Chance.'

Legacy

'Foolish' shares the title for the longest-reigning Hot 100 hit by a woman in her first chart appearance as a lead artist (tied with Debby Boone's 1977 single 'You Light Up My Life'). *Billboard* also ranked 'Foolish' No. 19 on its decade-end chart that looked at the most successful songs of the 2000s.

Remixes

The official remix features vocals from The Notorious B.I.G., including a verse lifted from the 1997 R. Kelly collaboration 'Fuck You Tonight.' Elsewhere, the UK CD single release included a Topnotch Remix of 'Foolish.'

Covers

- **2021, Moneybagg Yo -** The Memphis rapper sampled the song for his ode to vices, 'Wockesha Remix,' which also featured new vocals from Ashanti.

SZA

Depending on who you ask, SZA shouldn't be in this book. *See.SZA. Run*, SZA's 2012 debut EP, introduced an artist who was in no way, shape or form committed to a genre. The singer-songwriter has been fighting against labels since the very beginning – tagging *See.SZA.Run* and her follow-up EP, 2013's *S*, as "Alternative" and even more specifically "indie," "abstract," "atmospheric" and the creative "glitter trap." None of these descriptions are wrong.

"The only reason I'm defined as an R&B artist is because I'm Black," SZA candidly told *Dazed* in 2024. "It's almost a little reductive because it doesn't allow space to be anything else or try anything else. Justin Bieber is not considered an R&B artist; he is a pop artist who makes R&B, folk music, or whatever his heart desires. I simply just want to be allowed the same opportunity to make whatever I want without a label, [without it being] based on the colour of my skin, or the crew that I run with, or the beats that I choose."

Even in the early days, SZA's approach ran the gamut of sound and style, existing within the grounded realm of rhythm and blues as comfortably as the shimmering world of pop. As SZA has progressed within her career during the past decade, she has loosened her grip on the wheel of categorization. SZA finally welcomed the R&B label with open arms on 'Snooze', released on the critically and commercially successful 2022 album *SOS*. Originally conceived as a duet with legendary R&B hitmaker Babyface for his 2022 woman-dominant album *Girls Night Out*, the collaboration instead landed in SZA's lap. SZA, a fiercely independent and competitive songwriter, handled the lyrics and melodies herself, while the music was a collective effort between Babyface, the production team of The Rascals (R&B auteur Leon Thomas and producer Khris Riddick-Tynes) and Blair Ferguson a.k.a. BLK, who first built the foundation of the song in a demo.

The lyrical atmosphere of amorous adoration and devoted dedication, fused with the swirling, sensuous soundscape, combined to form a song that was a sleeper hit. Initially debuting at No. 29 on the Billboard Hot 100 in December 2022, 'Snooze' spent months on the chart as a beloved album cut – until the song was officially promoted on radio. From that moment, 'Snooze' ascended the chart, eventually peaking at No. 2. The song spent 70 weeks in total on the Hot 100, making it the only song to chart for the entire year in 2023. At the 2024 Grammys, 'Snooze' won Best R&B Song, solidifying SZA as an established contributor to

> **The only reason I'm defined as an R&B artist is because I'm Black.**
>
> **SZA**

the genre. In April 2024, Spotify selected 'Snooze' as the greatest R&B song of the streaming era. Weeks after Spotify's declaration, SZA confessed that she wasn't always the biggest fan of the song, despite its proven success. "I'm not gon lie snooze wasn't my favorite when I made the album but now it's my favorite hands down," she wrote on Twitter/X on 24 April 2024. "Played it at the beach and it was noiiiiiiiceeeee. I'm late but thank y'all for riding til I got some sense."

Born Solána Imani Rowe in 1989 in St Louis, Missouri, SZA was raised in Maplewood, New Jersey, also the hometown of Ms. Lauryn Hill. SZA's mother was an executive at AT&T, while her father was an editor

SZA fully embraced R&B through her hit song 'Snooze', which Spotify selected as the greatest R&B song of the streaming era.

and producer at CNN. Living in the "quietly affluent" town of Maplewood, with esteemed and successful parents, SZA was afforded opportunities like competitive gymnastics training and cheerleading. These experiences doubled as both a blessing and a curse. "I went to school with all white kids, and in my Girl Scout troop, everyone was white," SZA told *Complex* in 2013. "I was being the token Black every day."

In addition to her race setting her apart from her peers and classmates, SZA was raised orthodox Muslim. She described her upbringing as "very sheltered, very conservative," involving wearing a hijab and her father heavily restricting her access to television and the radio. As such, her early exposure to music was shaped by her father's taste – he preferred Miles Davis, Billie Holiday, Louis Armstrong and other jazz giants. SZA's encounters with other types of music were unplanned or unexpected: she has a half-sister who introduced her to Lil Jon by way of an answering machine; one of SZA's classmates had a bat mitzvah, where she was gifted a mixtape that held songs by the Red Hot Chili Peppers, LFO and Macy Gray. Her exploration of music expanded further out when she found a partially broken iPod in gymnastics camp. Through the device, SZA became familiar with artists like Common, Björk, Wu-Tang Clan, Nas, Yasiin Bey (formerly known as Mos Def) and Jay-Z.

SZA first tried her hand at singing on a song with her brother, who raps under the name Manhattan. "The first time I ever sang, he was doing this song called 'Where Do We Go From Here', and he was like, 'Come sing,'" SZA recalled to *Complex*. "I don't even know why he asked me to do that. 'What do I say?' 'Say whatever you feel.' I sang these notes and when I heard it back I was like, "This doesn't sound so bad."" SZA's interest in being a performer swelled little by little, eventually leading her to sing informally onstage with the production duo Christian Rich;

she chose Amy Winehouse's 'Me and Mr Jones'. The reaction to her voice was overwhelmingly positive, with even those closest to SZA being shocked by her raw talent. She formed her stage name using the Supreme Alphabet of the Five Percent Nation – similar to RZA and GZA of the Wu-Tang Clan, the last two letters in her name stand for 'Zig-Zag' and 'Allah', while the first letter 'S' typically means "saviour," or in SZA's less egomaniacal, self-appointed definition, "sovereign."

Similar to RZA and GZA of the Wu-Tang Clan, SZA formed her stage name using the Supreme Alphabet of the Five Percent Nation.

SZA

In a serendipitous moment in 2011, SZA met Top Dawg Entertainment (TDE) co-president Terrence 'Punch' Henderson at Gramercy Theatre in New York City. Punch was attending the CMJ music festival in support of TDE's bubbling artist Kendrick Lamar, who had a showcase at the event. SZA, meanwhile, was representing a streetwear brand and promised to gift the TDE team with free swag. As luck would have it, she got the sizes wrong, but her music ended up saving the day. SZA had brought a girlfriend along with her to the event, who was listening to SZA's music in headphones while she talked to Punch. "I heard her friend just jammin', and was like, 'What's she listening to? She's not even listening to what we're saying!'" Punch told *Red Bull* in May 2014. Intrigued, he grabbed the headphones and listened – only to be impressed. "If she'd done that

> **I sang these notes and when I heard it back I was like, 'This doesn't sound so bad.'**
>
> **SZA**

'listen to my demo [thing],' we probably wouldn't be sitting here." While SZA wasn't signed to TDE right away, she began to form a bond with Punch, who would give her feedback on new songs and check in when he was in the area.

Still focused on carving out her own sound, SZA unintentionally went to work on her first project, 2012's *See.SZA.Run*. The EP is airy and ambient, at times hard-hitting, with production handled by aspiring beatmakers like Brandun DeShay and APSuperProducer. "*See.SZA.Run* was totally accidental," SZA told *Billboard* in 2013. "I just recorded one song, and then another, and then it was like, 'You should probably record some other songs and make something out of it.'" The lyrics on

A chance meeting with Terrence 'Punch' Henderson of Top Dawg Entertainment led to a budding mentorship that eventually transformed into a cosign deal for SZA, who also signed with RCA.

the EP were a moment of significant foreshadowing: from track one, SZA addresses the anxieties of her life, be they self-inflicted or thrust upon her. She's focused on controlling what she can, when she can, and that specifically is her unguarded approach to crafting music.

Her method of constructing the lines of her songs is where SZA shined early, her words and phrases taking on different meanings as she stacks concepts on top of concepts. She continued to build on her unconventional storytelling skills with *S*, released in 2013, and 2014's *Z*, which was her first release under TDE. With production handled by Mac Miller, under his Larry Fisherman alter ego ('Ur', 'Warm Winds'), Emile Haynie ('Green Mile', 'Shattered Ring', 'Omega'), and other hot producers of the moment (Toro y Moi, 'HiiiJack'), SZA set out to further hone her sound. Where her earlier EPs focused on capturing the ephemeral feeling of being a millennial finding her way, *Z* was a window

On her early EPs, SZA preferred an abstract songwriting approach, opting for lyrical depth and complex concepts.

into the direction SZA wanted to take her storytelling in the future. 'Ur', the opening track, is an immediate introduction to her lyrical acrobatics. The standouts of *Z* are 'Childs Play' featuring Chance the Rapper and 'Babylon' with Kendrick Lamar; here, the MCs up the ante lyrically and energetically to match SZA's idiosyncratic standards.

Post-*Z*, SZA began recording songs for her debut album. As she worked, she reached deep into her now-revered songwriting bag, lending her pen to superstar artists like Nicki Minaj and Beyoncé ('Feeling Myself'), Travis Scott ('Ok Alright') and Rihanna ('Consideration'). She also worked alongside her TDE labelmates on their diverse projects, from Schoolboy Q's 2016 gangsta rap album *Blank Face* ('Neva Change') to Kendrick Lamar's freewheeling, uninhibited 2016 album *untitled unmastered* ('untitled 04 | 08.14.2014.'). Despite her ample works with TDE, SZA began to express concerns about the way the label was handling her debut. In October of 2016, she tweeted: "I actually quit. [Punch] can release my album if he ever feels like it. Y'all be blessed." She quickly deleted the tweet, but her frustrations with a lack of progress on her material were made clear.

In spring 2017, SZA was signed to RCA Records in a cosign deal with TDE. By June, she had released her highly anticipated album *Ctrl*, which recalibrated any and all expectations that any fans, old or new, may have held. With this project, SZA dropped the abstract pretences and dove headfirst into vulnerable songwriting, a decision that had instant benefits. Whether she was stringing together thoughts about her insecurities ('Supermodel', 'Normal Girl') or addressing her take on mortality ('20 Something'), SZA made it clear that she was in the business of weaving together relatable tales.

While *Ctrl* is built to be a genre-averse experience, mostly vacillating between indie-alternative and pop, the songs that connected most with listeners were the R&B tracks. 'The Weekend' sees SZA staking her claim on a taken man and 'Broken Clocks' addresses the slippery nature of time

SZA

and schedules – both of these songs were produced by ThankGod4Cody, a frequent collaborator of SZA's. With its multipronged approach, *Ctrl* easily made its way to five times platinum, with 'The Weekend' hitting seven times platinum and 'Broken Clocks' hitting six times platinum. The soul and grit of these songs have become SZA's foundation, on which she would continue constructing new material.

In August 2020, SZA again expressed her disdain toward TDE, and the following month, she made her long-awaited return as a lead artist with 'Hit Different' featuring Ty Dolla Sign and production from The Neptunes. On Christmas of that year, she dropped 'Good Days', which was teased at the end of the 'Hit Different' music video. Her fans gravitated strongly toward 'Good Days', a top 10 hit in New Zealand, Australia, Ireland, Malaysia, Lithuania, Singapore and the US, which focused on looking toward the future and moving past present

Soul, grit and raw vulnerability powered SZA's critically acclaimed, five-times platinum debut album, *Ctrl*.

negativity; it has since been certified eight times platinum. In late 2021 and 2022, SZA continued to drop music as teasers ('I Hate U', 'Shirt') before releasing the tracks outright, which generated attention and excitement amongst her fans.

In December 2022, SZA released *SOS*, her follow-up to the successful *Ctrl*, which included 'Good Days', 'I Hate U' and 'Shirt'. Continuing her tradition of not wanting to be beholden to one genre, SZA used *SOS* to explore alternative, pop, hip-hop and, of course, R&B. 'Kill Bill', a deceptively simple pop&B record, is yet again an example of SZA's vivid storytelling on full display. Its clarity worked: 'Kill Bill' became SZA's first No. 1 on the Billboard Hot 100 and Global 200 charts. *SOS* spent its first seven weeks atop the Billboard 200, the longest run for a woman artist since the mega-pop star Taylor Swift's 2020 album *folklore*; it also became the first R&B album to sit at No. 1 for that stretch of time since Whitney Houston's 1987 album *Whitney*.

SOS has since been certified six times platinum and it nabbed the 2024 Grammy for Best Progressive R&B Album. In December 2024,

---

SZA

ALBUMS:
Ctrl (2017)
SOS (2022)

SONGS:
'Babylon' featuring Kendrick Lamar (2014)
'Ur' (2014)
'Childs Play' featuring Chance the Rapper (2014)
'ScHoolboy Q, Neva Change' (2016)
'untitled 04 | 08.14.2014' Kendrick Lamar (2016)
'Love Galore' featuring Travis Scott (2017)
'The Weekend' (2017)
'Broken Clocks' (2017)
'All the Stars' with Kendrick Lamar (2018)
'Hit Different' (2020)
'Good Days' (2020)
'I Hate U' (2021)
'Shirt' (2022)
'Kill Bill' (2023)
'Snooze' (2023)
'Saturn' (2024)
'Luther' with Kendrick Lamar (2024)

Despite her ongoing struggles with fame and anxiety, SZA continues to defy expectations – and genres.

SZA released *Lana*, the deluxe edition of *SOS*, which yielded the lush lead single 'Saturn'. The song went on to win Best R&B Performance at the 2025 Grammys. "She has the answers to some of the things she was curious about and is willing to tell it all in the most disruptive yet beautiful compositions this generation has ever heard," her longtime collaborator Kendrick Lamar succinctly told *British Vogue* in a December 2024 issue. The year 2025 saw their collaboration 'Luther' hit No. 1 on the Billboard Hot 100 immediately followed by SZA supporting Lamar on his stadium tour, the Grand National Tour.

"Every day I grapple with, "Am I done with music?"" SZA mused in the same *British Vogue* interview. "Maybe I'm just not meant to be famous – I'm crashing and burning and behaving erratically. It's not for me because I have so much anxiety. But why would God put me in this position if I wasn't supposed to be doing this? So I just keep trying to rise to the occasion. But I'm also just like, 'Please … the occasion is beating my ass.'"

SZA, 'SNOOZE'

Release date: April 25, 2023
Album: *SOS*
Recorded: 2021
Label: Top Dawg Entertainment
Studio: n/a
Songwriters: Solána 'SZA' Rowe,
Kenneth 'Babyface' Edmonds, Khris
Riddick-Tynes, Leon Thomas, Blair
Ferguson
Billboard Hot 100: 2
UK Singles Chart: 18

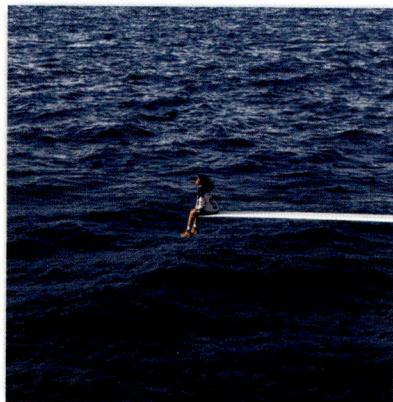

Critical Acclaim

After years of fighting against being boxed into a genre, SZA finally welcomed the R&B label with open arms on 'Snooze', released on the critically and commercially successful 2022 album *SOS*. The lyrical atmosphere of amorous adoration and devoted dedication, combined with the swirling, sensuous soundscape, combined to form a song that was a sleeper hit.

Recording

Originally conceived as a duet with legendary R&B hitmaker Babyface for his 2022 woman-dominant album *Girls Night Out*, the collaboration instead landed in SZA's lap. She handled the lyrics and melodies herself, while the music was a collective effort between Babyface, the production team of The Rascals (R&B auteur Leon Thomas and producer Khris Riddick-Tynes) and Blair Ferguson, a.k.a. BLK, who first built the foundation of the song in a demo.

Legacy

Initially debuting at No. 29 on the *Billboard* Hot 100 in December 2022, 'Snooze' spent months on the chart as a beloved album cut before it was officially promoted on radio. From then on, 'Snooze' climbed the chart, eventually peaking at No. 2. The song spent 70 weeks in total on the Hot 100, charting for the entirety of 2023 – the only song that year to do so. At the 2024 Grammys, 'Snooze' won Best R&B Song, solidifying SZA's status as an established contributor to the genre. In April 2024, Spotify selected 'Snooze' as the greatest R&B song of the streaming era.

Remixes

Justin Bieber is featured in an acoustic duet with SZA on the official 'Snooze' remix.

Covers

- **2023, Joseph Solomon -** The Texas singer-songwriter performed a cover that has reached over 2 million views on YouTube.
- **2024, Baekhyun -** The South Korean singer and actor shared his version to YouTube, where it has been viewed more than 1 million times.

H.E.R.

Guitar virtuoso and R&B singer-songwriter H.E.R. officially began her career in 2016, upon the release of her debut EP, *H.E.R. Vol. 1.* So many accolades came from that moment that the world wanted to know how her singing and songwriting had begun. When her music first hit the masses, very little about H.E.R. was known.

The only available image was the cover photo of the aforementioned EP, which featured a glowing silhouette of H.E.R. against a blue backdrop. It wasn't long though before listeners began to put the pieces together; most notably, her soulful cover of Drake's 2015 song 'Jungle' was premiered via *Complex* under the name Gabi Wilson and a reworked version later appeared on *H.E.R. Vol. 1*. Despite the relatively short amount of time being 100 per cent anonymous, H.E.R. held onto the concept until she couldn't anymore. "I definitely had a feeling it was gonna happen but I didn't think people were going to dig that deep into that," H.E.R. told *Billboard* in December 2016. "I didn't think they would care as much. People are gonna listen to the music whether or not I reveal myself."

Living my truth was very hard – I felt vulnerable.

H.E.R.

Born Gabriella Sarmiento Wilson in 1997, in Vallejo, California, H.E.R. showed early signs of musical prowess. After growing up in a home environment brimming with instrumentally and vocally gifted artists, H.E.R. picked up the family trade, playing several instruments including the piano, drums, guitar and bass. She started writing poetry and making music at five years old, and by age 10 she had performed Alicia Keys' 'If I Ain't Got You' and 'No One' on the *Today Show* and Aretha Franklin's 'Freeway of Love' at *Showtime at the Apollo* under the name Gabi Wilson, impressing the adult hosts with her precociousness, bona fide talent and serious career mindset. Additional performances came soon after, including appearances on *Maury* in 2007 and, the following year, *Good Morning America* and *The View*. At age 12, H.E.R. performed briefly at the 2010 BET Awards, covering Alicia Keys' 'Fallin'.' In 2011, aged 14, she signed a deal with MBK Entertainment/J

Records, which then merged with RCA, making H.E.R. Alicia Keys' labelmate – a surreal situation after H.E.R. spent her entire childhood covering Keys' music.

In 2014, H.E.R. released her debut single, 'Something to Prove', under her real name, a boom-bap heavy love song that deftly sampled The Isley Brothers' 'Between the Sheets'. Not long after issuing this single, and premiering the 2015 'Jungle' cover, H.E.R. took a step back, choosing to cloak herself in mystery instead of presenting herself as the child prodigy she had come to be known as. "Living my truth was very hard – I felt vulnerable,' H.E.R. told *The Guardian* in November 2018. 'Some people ask me: 'Is it an alter ego, is it another version of yourself?' But it's just my inner self. It's all the thoughts and feelings that sit in the back of my mind and I'm afraid to say."

H.E.R. officially began her career in 2016 with the enigmatic release of *H.E.R. Vol. 1*, but her prodigious musical talent had long been on display, dating back to her childhood.

H.E.R.

H.E.R. stands for "having everything revealed," an ironic acronym given the presentation, but becoming H.E.R. wasn't just about being an enigma. It was about controlling her expression of self, which included coming face to face with the inevitability of human error. "The music, I think for me, it's the evolution of woman," H.E.R. told *NPR* in December 2016. "And I feel like throughout, let's say, my teenage years, I've made mistakes and I've felt like I'm the only one that has done that or I feel bad about this or I fell for the wrong guy – never thought I would fall for the wrong guy. I never thought I would be that girl, and I became H.E.R. That's kind of how the concept came to be."

With a new stage name, plus an extensive collection of disguising sunglasses, H.E.R. released her debut EP in September 2016, produced by David 'Swagg R'Celious' Harris and Darhyl 'Hey DJ' Camper Jr, along with other contributors. Driven by a covert mission to deliver the message with less focus on the messenger, *H.E.R. Vol. 1* breathes in relational imperfections and breathes out open vulnerability and acceptance. "*Vol. 1* was a collection of songs that represented the time I was transitioning from a young girl to a young woman," H.E.R. told *Grammy.com* in August 2018. "It turned into a very selfless thing because many women can now relate to it."

'Focus', a double platinum, dreamy effort that sees H.E.R. singing ethereally over delicate harp, caught the attention of Rihanna, who posted an Instagram video of herself in April 2017 with 'Focus' as the background song. "I was shocked but excited when I saw the video she made, which lowkey fits perfectly lol," she told *The Fader* over email in April 2017. "I have always been a huge Rihanna fan, even did a cover to 'Yeah, I Said It' a few months ago. I am beyond humbled that she listens to my music. The fact that she posted it was surreal. God is great!" H.E.R.'s visibility increased tenfold after this shoutout, which reached more than six million views, making it even more difficult to remain anonymous.

Ironically, H.E.R. is an acronym for 'having everything revealed'.

> **It was almost like I was forced to reveal myself – like, 'OK, it's time.'**
>
> **H.E.R.**

But H.E.R. forged ahead with the mission, releasing *Vol. 2* in June 2017, continuing the amorous theme she first introduced in *Vol. 1*. The platinum certified 'Every Kind Of Way', a warm, inviting track that billows with the overwhelming desire for one's romantic partner, immediately connected with listeners. "Being anonymous, I thought I'd just release the music and see what happens organically," H.E.R. told the *Los Angeles Times* in July 2017. "It hasn't even been a year and everything is happening so fast. It was almost like I was forced to reveal myself – like, 'OK, it's time.'"

In August 2017, Daniel Caesar released a wholesome duet with H.E.R. titled 'Best Part', which reached No. 1 on the US Adult R&B Songs chart on Billboard and No. 21 on the Philippines Hot 100. It has since been certified six times platinum, underscoring the dulcet theme of mutual

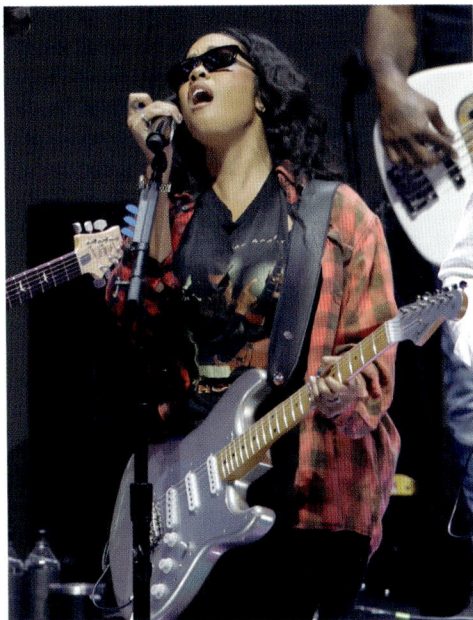

admiration. 'Best Part', also a Grammy Award winner for Best R&B Performance, was placed on the compilation album *H.E.R.*, which was released in October 2017 and joined volumes 1 and 2, in addition to six new tracks. The collection reached No. 1 on the Top R&B/Hip-Hop Albums Billboard chart, won Best R&B Album at the 2019 Grammys and H.E.R. was nominated in the Big Four categories of Album of the Year and Best New Artist.

By the end of 2017, H.E.R.'s identity was all but revealed, but the talent far outweighed the discovery. "It's not even about the glamour and the crazy personality any more," H.E.R. told *The Guardian*. "It's just about what do you make me feel with your music and your words. [It's about] all the underdogs, the people who weren't the most popular in school or the people who were told they weren't gonna be anything. But they really have a story to show the world and people can identify with them." *I Used to Know Her: The Prelude* followed in August 2018, led by the slow-burning, double platinum Bryson Tiller collaboration 'Could've Been', which powered the project to No. 1 on the Top R&B/Hip-Hop Albums Billboard chart. "A lot of the songs have just come from this place of wanting to elevate, bring out more musicality, and do things more freely," H.E.R. told *Elle* magazine in September 2018. "*I Used to Know H.E.R.* is my perspective in life up to this point: all the things I've experienced, all my stories, those things that really have built who I am.

H.E.R.'s mysterious identity was short-lived, but her talent far outweighed the discovery.

H.E.R.

The title comes from how people who knew me in high school, who would push me aside or maybe disregard me and consider me a nobody, are now like: 'I used to know her.' They say that a lot." *I Used to Know Her: Part 2* came out in November 2018 and a compilation album of both volumes was released in August 2019.

With her debut studio album, *Back of My Mind* released in June 2021, H.E.R. finally shook off the mystery, a sliver of light highlighting a glimpse of her face on the cover. The lead single 'Slide' featured the West Coast rapper YG and was released that September; a remix featuring a who's who of some of the era's most popular artists (Pop Smoke, A Boogie wit da Hoodie, Chris Brown) was released in January 2020, boosting the song's popularity to triple platinum status. In a reaction to the 25 May 2020 police killing of unarmed African American man George Floyd, H.E.R. released 'I Can't Breathe', a cinematic, sorrowful song that reflects on the hardships Black people experience. It went on to win Song of the Year at the 2021 Grammys, a highly coveted award – but in H.E.R.'s words, 'I Can't Breathe' came from an unpretentious place. "I didn't really think, 'I'm going to write a song about this,' but I [started] catching up with my friend who I write with a lot," H.E.R. told *People* magazine in March 2021. "She's like my big sister here, and we were just having a conversation about everything going on. Like, 'Isn't this crazy? What can we do?' We're saying all these things, and I had my guitar in my hands. The song kind of just happened. I started singing, 'I can't breathe, you're taking my life from me.' And it all just came organically. It was easy to write because of everything that was flowing."

'Damage', the follow-up single released in October, liberally sampled Jimmy Jam & Terry Lewis's production on Herb Alpert's 1987 single 'Making Love in the Rain'. With a heartfelt plea to be handled with care,

H.E.R. expanded her sound further with the release of the Grammy Award-winning protest anthem 'I Can't Breathe.'

'Damage' touched the emotions of anyone who's ever had a romantic interaction, leading to a platinum certification and a No. 1 hit on R&B radio. In February 2021, H.E.R. contributed 'Fight for You' to *Judas and the Black Messiah: The Inspired Album*. Cowritten with fellow singer-songwriter Tiara Thomas and co-composed with producer D'Mile, the song is a contemplative groove that sees H.E.R. pining for freedom. 'Fight for You', with its haunting melodies and uplifting verses, won the Academy Award for Best Original Song, in addition to a Grammy for Best Traditional R&B Performance. At the first Children's and Family Emmys in 2022, H.E.R. took home the award for Outstanding Short Form Program for the Obama-produced Netflix animated series *We the People*, a programme H.E.R. wrote for, including the inspiring song 'Change'.

With multiple Grammy Awards, an Oscar and an Emmy under her belt, H.E.R. is just one more award – a Tony – away from EGOT status. It's an appropriate trajectory for an artist who has been fighting for her music to be heard unfettered – but as her career has unfolded, H.E.R. has become more open to the idea of being seen. That includes starring roles in films like a live-action rendition of *Beauty and the Beast* and a supporting role in the remake of *The Color Purple*. 'I've been re-finding my voice,' the artist said in a statement to *Vibe* magazine

H.E.R.

ALBUMS:
H.E.R. (2017)
I Used to Know Her (2019)
Back of My Mind (2021)

SONGS:
'Something to Prove' (2014)
'Focus' (2016)
'Every Kind Of Way' (2017)
'Best Part' with Daniel Caesar (2017)
'Could've Been' featuring Bryson Tiller (2018)
'Slide' featuring YG (2019)
'Jhene Aiko, B.S.' (2020)
'I Can't Breathe' (2020)
'Damage' (2020)
'Fight for You' (2021)
'Change' (2021)
'Come Through' featuring Chris Brown (2021)

in December 2022. "Now I'm not wearing glasses. I can't be acting and wearing glasses, so I think it's time for people to really get to know the person behind H.E.R. H.E.R. is me, but at the same time, it's a new chapter of my life, and I think I'm really finding that connection, and I'm allowing people to see under the layers a little bit."

H.E.R. has evolved from a mysterious musical force to an award-winning, multidimensional artist who embraces visibility.

H.E.R., 'DAMAGE'

Release date: October 21, 2020
Album: *Back of My Mind*
Recorded: n/a
Label: RCA
Studio: n/a
Songwriters: Gabriella 'H.E.R.' Wilson, Tiara Thomas, Ant Clemons, Carl 'Cardiak' McCormick, Jeff 'Gitty' Gitelman, James 'Jimmy Jam' Harris III, Terry Lewis
Billboard Hot 100: 44
UK Singles Chart: 100

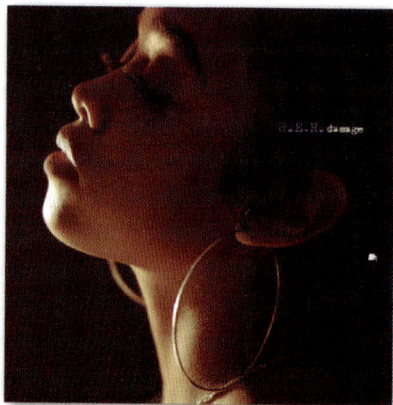

Critical Acclaim

Released after 'I Can't Breathe', the heartrending ode to George Floyd, an unarmed African American man killed by police, 'Damage' sees H.E.R. leaning into another side of her vulnerability.

Recording

Produced by Cardiak and Gitty, 'Damage' liberally sampled Jimmy Jam & Terry Lewis's production on Herb Alpert's 1987 single 'Making Love in the Rain'.

Legacy

With a heartfelt plea to be handled with care, 'Damage' touched the emotions of anyone who's ever had a romantic interaction, leading to a platinum certification and a No. 1 hit on R&B radio.

Remixes

Electronic beatsmith Kaytranada remixed the song with downtempo dancehall elements. 'Damage' also received a high-energy Justin Credible Remix and a dance-driven Joel Corry Remix.

Covers

- **2023, Terrace Martin -** The composer, producer and multi-instrumentalist recorded a jazz-influenced version on his album *Fine Tune.*

SOURCES

Aaliyah.com, *ABC News, AllMusic, Allure, Andscape,* Associated Press, *Ashanti: The Making of a Star* (documentary) BET.com, *Billboard,* Biography.com, *Black Film, Blavity,* Britannica, *BuzzFeed,* CBS News, Chicago Tribune, Clash Music, *Complex,* Consequence.net, *Cosmopolitan, Dazed Digital,* E! *News, Ebony, Elle, Elle Canada, Entertainment Weekly, ESPN the Magazine, Essence, Extra TV, The FADER,* Fashionista.com, *Forbes, Fräulein Magazine, Genius,* Grammy.com, *The Guardian, Hip Online, Hip-Hop DX,* Huff Post, *The Independent, Interview Magazine, Janet Jackson.* (docuseries), KCRW, Library of Congress, *Los Angeles Times,* Mississippi Writers and Musicians, MTV, *Music Connection,* National Museum of African American History & Culture, New Jersey Hall of Fame, *New York Daily News, New York Magazine,* NPR, *Okayplayer, O* Magazine, *People,* Pitchfork, *Playbill, Pop Crush, Popsugar, RandBeing, Rated RnB,* Recording Industry Association of America, Red Bull, *Refinery29, Rolling Stone, Rome News-Tribune, Schön! Magazine,* The Smithsonian Center for Folklife and Cultural Heritage, Spotify Newsroom, *Spyscape, The Standard, Stereogum, The Telegraph, The Terrell Show, The Things, TIME, The Today Show, UDiscoverMusic, USA Today, Vanity Fair, Variety,* VH1, *VIBE Magazine, Vice, VOA News, Vogue UK, Vox, W Magazine, The Washington Post,* WCRZ.com, *Whitney: Can I Be Me* (documentary), WhitneyHouston. com, WorldRadioHistory.com, *You Know I Got Soul,* YouTube interviews (*ABC iview; All Access*; Angie Martinez IRL; Apple Music; *Ashanti: The Making of A Star;* BBC Breakfast; BET Awards; CNN; *Entertainment Tonight; Extra TV; Genius*; Grammy Awards; *The Music Factory; The Oprah Winfrey Show; Plus Vite Que La Musique*; Rock & Roll Hall of Fame; *Showtime at the Apollo; Soul Train; The Source: All Access*; Star Sessions; *The Today Show; The Tonight Show*; TV One; VERZUZ; *Video Music Box*)

Books:

Gerrick Kennedy, *Didn't We Almost Have it All: In Defense of Whitney Houston* (Abrams, 2022); Kathy Iandoli, *Baby Girl: Better Known as Aaliyah* (Atria Books, 2021)

PHOTO
CREDITS

p1 dpa picture alliance/Alamy; p4 Hulton Archive/Getty; p7 Michael Ochs Archives/Getty; p9 Michael Ochs Archives/Stringer/Getty; p10 Tom Copi/Michael Ochs Archives/Getty; p11 Michael Ochs Archives/Getty; p12 Gie Knaeps/Getty; p15 Harry Langdon/Getty; p17 Everett Collection Inc/Alamy; p13 Anthony Barboza/Getty; p19 Rob Verhorst/Redferns; p20 Pictorial Press Ltd/Alamy; p22 WENN Rights Ltd/Alamy; p25 Sven Hoogerhuis/BSR Agency via Getty; p27 United Archives GmbH/Alamy; p29 Jeff Haynes/AFP via Getty; p30 Virgin Records/Universal Music Group; p33 Christian Rose/Roger Viollet via Getty; p35 Jack Mitchell/Getty; p37 Gary Gershoff/Getty; p38 CBW/Alamy; p40 colaimages/Alamy; p41 Goedefroit Music/Getty; p42 Michael Zagaris/Getty; p44 PA Images/Alamy; p47 Bob Riha, Jr./Getty; p48 Arista/Colombia Pictures Industries Inc/Sony Music Entertainment; p51 Pictorial Press Ltd/Alamy; p53 Allstar Picture Library/Alamy; p55 PictureLux/The Hollywood Archive/Alamy; p56 Ernie Pollard/Alamy; p59 Robert Hoetink/Alamy; p60 LANDMARK MEDIA/Alamy; p62 *Glitter* productions/Lauren Mark Prod/Maroon Ent/20th/Columbia/Macauley, Bruce/Album/Alamy; p65 John Atashian/Alamy; p66 Island Def Jam Music Group/Universal Music Group; p69 dpa picture alliance/Alamy; p70 JEP Live Music/Alamy; p72 USAID/Alamy; p75 Michael Walker/Alamy; p75 Michael Walker/Alamy; p76 MediaPunch Inc/Alamy; p76 The Syndicate/Alamy; p78 The Syndicate/Alamy; p80 MCA Records/Universal Music Group; p83 Raymond Boyd/Getty; p94 Blackground Entertainment/Virgin Records America; p85 Catherine McGann/Getty; p87 Kevin Mazur/WireImage via Getty; p89 KMazur/WireImage via Getty; p91 Sal Idriss/Redferns via Getty; p93 Hector Mata/AFP via Getty; p96 David Corio/Getty; p99 Pictorial Press Ltd/Alamy; p101 Sonia Moskowitz/Getty; p103 Raymond Boyd/Getty; p104 Simon Meaker/Alamy; p107 MediaPunch Inc/Alamy; p109 Raymond Boyd/Getty; p110 Atlantic Recording Corporation; p113 dpa picture alliance/Alamy;

p114 Brittany Smith/Alamy; p116 Smiley N. Pool/Houston Chronicle via Getty; p117 Everett Collection Inc/Alamy; p119 Everett Collection Inc/Alamy; p120 Pam Francis/Liaison; p123 Barry King/Alamy; p125 Christopher Polk/Getty; p126 Colombia Records/Sony Music Entertainment; p129 Associated Press/Alamy; p130 US Air Force Photo/Alamy; p132 Francis Specker/Alamy; p134 PA Images/Alamy; p136 US Air Force Photo/Alamy; p137 Timothy A. Clary/AFP via Getty; p139 PA Images/Alamy; p140 Murder Inc Records/Def Jam Recordings Republic Corps; p143 Associated Press/Alamy; p145 John Parra/Getty Images for Revolt Music Conference; p149 ZUMA Press, Inc./Alamy; p149 Harry Durrant/Getty; p150 Christopher Polk/Billboard via Getty; p152 Associated Press/Alamy; p153 David Moffly/Alamy; p155 Lawrey/Alamy; p156 Top Dawg Entertainment/RCA/Sony Music Entertainment; p159 Bennett Raglin/Getty; p161 Robby Klein/Getty; p162 Jeff Kravitz/FilmMagic; p164 Ezra Shaw/Getty; p166 Kevin Mazur/Getty Images for Global Citizen; p167 Kevin Winter/Getty Images for Crossroads Guitar Festival; p169 Ezra Shaw/Getty Images; p171 Daniel Shirey/MLB Photos via Getty; p172 RCA/Sony Music Entertainment